RELATIONSHIPS MATTER

"If you have ever been intrigued by the mysteries of gender parity at the top, and what it takes to have a fulfilling career without losing yourself in the journey, this book is a must. Drawing from decades of experience working with amazing women, Dr. Rosina Racioppi gets to the core of the stumbling blocks holding women back and unveils the secrets behind each one of them. By the time you get to the last page, you'll have fresh insights about why *Relationships Matter*—and you'll know how to build and leverage yours for success!"

Marta Vallejo Mestres
Justice and Human Rights Specialist
United Nations Development Programme (UNDP)

"Dr. Rosina Racioppi is a credible authority in explaining the power of effective networking. This book caused me to reflect on the fact that active networking is not manipulative, but actually authentic. Leveraging your curiosity about people—their experiences, values, and beliefs—helps to expand and hone your own point of view. And, by sharing those new insights and seeking to understand those of others, you learn to influence people unlike yourself and enhance the inclusivity and productivity of your organization. *Relationships Matter* will help women build the confidence and skills to make themselves both savvy and successful."

Cindy Lowden
Senior Vice President
Human Resources Business Partnerships

"*Relationships Matter* by Dr. Rosina Racioppi is a brilliant book on a core topic. The book uncovers an amazing approach to developing a strong network and building and leveraging relationships. A relationship can even start with just small talk or feedback taken in constructive and positive ways. The book will help to encourage all to make relationships meaningful, and even inspirational."

Edie Fraser
Managing Director
Diversified Search

"Dr. Rosina Racioppi's new book, *Relationships Matter: How Women Use Developmental Networks to Step into Their Power and Influence*, is full of practical and relevant insights to help talented women at any level think through a strategy to accelerate their development and career satisfaction. Informed by years of focusing on advancing women in business, Dr. Racioppi uses the art of storytelling and reflection to package sage advice for tomorrow's women leaders. It is a great read for women and men alike."

Daniel Marsili
SVP and Chief Human Resources Officer
Colgate-Palmolive Company

"It's easy as a female leader to give lip service to the importance of building relationships and establishing your value proposition. Dr. Rosina Racioppi teaches you how to be accountable to yourself to actually get out there and do it. *Relationships Matter* is a must-read for leaders at all levels."

Carolyn A. Wiesenhahn
Senior HR Executive
CVS Health

"This book is an invaluable resource for every professional woman who has kept her head down, worked hard, and found herself passed over for opportunities. The truth is, we're social creatures at heart, and we all need each other in innumerable ways. Avoiding networking opportunities because you don't want to get involved in politics or put yourself out there will lead to your great work being overlooked every time. Dr. Rosina Racioppi's combination of personal stories, research, and practical how-to tips will help move your career forward."

Diana Thomas
Executive Coach, Advisor, and Author
Winning Results, LLC

"Dr. Rosina Racioppi answers the why, how, and what around developing business relationships. This book contains those critical points around networking and building your own Board of Directors, which are crucial to professional growth. This is the stuff they don't teach you in school! Excellent read with practical approaches that you can implement now."

Dovie Majors
General Manager
Amazon

"Each page in *Relationships Matter* provides tools and insights to help you build a lasting network. It doesn't matter what stage you are at in your career; a book like this reiterates the importance of building a network. Through the stories and examples shared in this book, Dr. Rosina Racioppi gives you the tools to build relationships that really matter."

Dr. Douglas Clayton
Senior Vice President
HC Leadership Americas & Leadership Development

RELATIONSHIPS
MATTER

HOW WOMEN USE
DEVELOPMENTAL NETWORKS
TO STEP INTO
THEIR POWER AND INFLUENCE

Dr. Rosina L. Racioppi

RELATIONSHIPS MATTER

HOW WOMEN USE DEVELOPMENTAL NETWORKS TO STEP INTO THEIR POWER AND INFLUENCE

To contact Rosina:

Website ...... https://www.women-unlimited.com/

Contact Us .. https://www.women-unlimited.com/contact-us/

LinkedIn ...... https://www.linkedin.com/company/women-unlimited/

Blog .... https://www.women-unlimited.com/blog/

Facebook ... https://www.facebook.com/womenunlimitedinc/

Twitter .... https://twitter.com/womenunlimited_ (@womenunlimited_)

To contact the publisher, inCredible Messages Press, visit www.inCredibleMessages.com.

Printed in the United States of America
ISBN 978-1-7322510-8-3

Book Strategists .... Bonnie Budzowski & Leslie Rubin

Cover Design .... Bobbie Fox Fratangelo

Dedication

This book is dedicated to women seeking to grow and advance and to the leaders who want to know how to guide them.

Acknowledgments

I have had the good fortune to understand, from a very young age, the importance of relationships. Growing up in a large family (my mother was one of 11 children), I witnessed my mother talking with other family members about various issues. While I knew she already had firm perspectives on these issues, I noticed that my mother was still curious to learn about others' perspectives as well.

When I asked her about this, my mother explained that she wanted to grow her understanding. Looking back, I see that this propensity shaped me significantly. My mother's influence was invaluable as I started my career because it informed how I formed relationships. Because I was working in human resources, it was important that I understood how the various business/department leaders viewed business challenges. Establishing relationships with others who were willing to express their views to me would play a key role in the success of my career.

In fact, two components of the learning framework used in WOMEN Unlimited Inc.'s (WUI's) programs focus on relationships: mentoring and networking. This is because relationships complement and deepen a woman's knowledge of how to make a dramatic difference in her career.

One of my mentors, Jack Yurish, whom you will meet in this book, reminds aspiring leaders that technical merit only gets you *in* the game. Relationships help to form and inform your thinking and understanding, which helps prepare you to address challenges. Relationships also help you understand how to navigate organizations to achieve goals and advance. Since business landscapes change and evolve so quickly, relationships are increasingly important.

For instance, I leveraged the power of relationships in order to write this book. The leaders who graciously agreed to participate in its research are individuals I have known through WUI, my research, and my work at the University of Pennsylvania. When I reached out and asked for their insights, each was supportive, and I commend how open they were in sharing their experiences—some of which are very personal. The stories these individuals shared about their growth are great resources for all of us to learn from.

Since 1994, WUI has partnered with organizations that desire to increase the number of women in leadership roles. Together, we seek to identify the contributing forces that will change the corporate landscape. As we learn and grow with our corporate partners, we discover their specific challenges in making our shared vision a reality. We also learn from the managers of women who participate in the program as well as from the senior men and women who participate as mentors. Through these various relationships, our work has grown and become more impactful year after year.

At its core, WUI is a learning organization, and, as an organization, we practice what we teach: we value our relationships with one another and learn from diverse perspectives. I appreciate how CFO and part-owner of WUI, Nina Dougar, continually provides valuable insight that helps guide and grow our organization. Her influence has helped strengthen WUI and distill the teachings imparted in this book.

You will meet two more of our leaders in these pages who graciously shared their insights and experiences. Global Vice President of Learning and Development, Amy Gonzales, has been a part of WUI since it launched in 1994. Amy has a passion for creating environments where people can learn and is perfectly suited for her position.

Vice President of Corporate Partner Relationships, Ann Calello Groccia, spent her early career at Fidelity Investments. You will learn how Ann grew to understand and be passionate about the power of relationships. Every day, I am grateful for what I learn from the wonderful community of women at WUI.

My one regret is that Jean Otte, my friend, mentor, and the founder of WUI, passed away before I could share my plan for writing this book. Jean's spirit and courage are on the pages of my life and every page of this book. I am grateful that Jean's friend and mentor, Jack Yurish, provided stories about Jean and how she launched WUI.

I also want to recognize the contribution of the women who participate in our programs and share their experience and vulnerability. Their contributions help us ensure that we are authentic, realistic, and practical. It's incredible to watch these women discover how to empower themselves and become leaders in their own organizations. Our relationships with these women enrich us all.

Like most big projects, creating a book "takes a village." In the case of this book, it took the book strategist team of Bonnie Budzowski and Leslie Rubin. Bonnie and Leslie were able to take my idea and help it become this book. Their talent and contribution not only made the project not only enjoyable, but also resulted in an exceptional outcome.

I am grateful to my wonderful husband, Fred, who helps me stay honest with myself and pushes me to continue to learn and grow. In our programs, we often discuss the importance of having a holistic view because we understand the harmony between our work and personal life, and in this regard, Fred is a big support. He helps me be the best mother I can be to my lovely daughters, Dina and Danielle, who have taught me more about myself than any other experience could have.

Contents

FOREWORD

R elationships have been a critical element in every success I've ever had. While I don't discount my education and hard work, I know I would never have made it as far as I have without my many supportive relationships. Let me share an example.

I was in the audience at a conference where Dr. Annie McKee, best-selling author and advisor to top global leaders, was speaking. I was mesmerized by McKee's presentation; she was completely focused and present with us in that moment. I just had to talk with her after the presentation.

As founder, publisher, and CEO of Diversity Woman Media, I host multiple conferences per year. More than anything, I wanted McKee to speak at one of those conferences. I was so focused on talking to her that, after powering my way to the front of the room, I accidentally interrupted as she talked with a high-profile woman who was hosting the conference.

Following that first conversation, I sent McKee copies of my magazine and reiterated my invitation. In addition to being a leadership consultant and prolific author, McKee is also a senior fellow at the University of Pennsylvania Graduate

School of Education. (She now teaches and leads the PennCLO Executive Doctoral Program and the Penn GSE Med Ed Master's Program.) With a jam-packed schedule even back then, McKee simply didn't have time to speak at one of my conferences. I extended the invitation several times, but it just didn't happen. But something else did.

Having heard a bit of my story through our conversations, McKee asked if she could interview me and include my story in a textbook she was writing. Of course, I was honored and quickly agreed. A year later, when the publisher wanted to redo the textbook, McKee contacted me again to ask if I would consent to a longer interview. I was delighted, and also determined to utilize this relationship to learn from her, an accomplished leader.

At the time of our longer interview, I was preparing to enter a doctoral program and was in the process of reviewing schools. I asked Annie McKee to give me her opinion of three schools I was considering. She responded, "If I were you, I'd consider the Chief Learning Officer doctorate program at the University of Pennsylvania. I'll write your recommendation." (At the time, McKee was on the board of directors. She later became director of the program.)

I was astounded. As an African American woman from the South, I had never expected to apply to an Ivy League school. Yet, that's what the power of relationships gave me the encouragement to do. I was accepted and earned my doctorate at the prestigious school.

This story of my relationship with Annie McKee is a perfect example of how relationships work. In making an introduction and staying in touch with this person I admired, I didn't initially get what I was looking for—a speaker for one of my conferences. I got something much more valuable, however, something McKee was happy to give. I, in turn, was more than happy to grant McKee the interviews she requested.

My relationship with Rosina Racioppi, author of the book you are holding, is an example as well. We started out as peers, both pursuing doctorates at Penn, seeing each other in classrooms. Then Rosina became a member of my dissertation committee, and I was more subordinate to her. Rosina knew I was having a rough time with other members of my committee, and her guidance and encouragement were invaluable to me.

Once we finished our doctorates, Rosina and I started collaborating to support each other's work. We looked at each other as industry peers, not as competitors but as collaborators. The networking we have done over the years has turned into something beautiful. Rosina made a heroic effort to show up when I won an entrepreneur award, and when she celebrated WOMEN Unlimited Inc.'s anniversary by ringing the bell at the New York stock exchange, she gave me credit for pushing her to think beyond her expectations.

I'm so excited about the book you are holding in your hands—because whatever obstacles might be impeding the growth of any woman's career, that woman has power to build a mutually supportive, growth-oriented network. She has the power to take ownership of her career.

In this book, Rosina not only makes the case that a network is essential, but she also shows her readers how to build one. In fact, she pulls back the curtain on how successful women leverage their networks to grow their careers. You'll love the tips, techniques, and stories showcased on these pages, including the story that belongs to Annie McKee!

Building a network is not passing out business cards. Rosina shows us that building relationships is a mindset, one that understands that valuable relationships are all around us. Valuable relationships include people who engage in conversations that help us think about things differently, who are available to answer our questions, can act as sounding boards, give advice, or provide ideas and insights that are different from our own. Latest research shows that the more diversity in your network (as in people who think, work, and live in ways dissimilar to you), the more powerful that network will be. When it comes to real growth, sameness is the enemy. That, of course, is music to my ears.

Networking relationships don't need to be forced, and they don't need to put you in one-down positions with others. For example, through a relationship, I once got the opportunity to sit down and have tea out of Dr. Maya Angelou's china, feature her on the cover of my magazine, and develop a relationship with her over time.

During my first conversation with this incredibly accomplished woman, I offered my help: "Is there ever anything I can do to be of assistance to you?"

We should never think that we are talking to people who don't want to have a mutually beneficial relationship. Even Oprah Winfrey wants to receive a birthday gift. We can't meet people and think that they have so much that we don't have anything to offer them.

Dr. Angelou continued to keep up with my work, and she sent an autographed portrait of herself as a gift to me, celebrating my conference anniversary. She encouraged me not to give up the work. And I have a painting on my wall that continues to bring me encouragement.

I love how Rosina reminds us that relationships aren't just something we seek to get, and we don't need to use relationships to play a game that compromises us. We seek to challenge and appreciate those ahead of us, we support our peers, and we invest in those who are coming after us. In every relationship, we are open, curious, and eager to give. In every relationship, we seek to be a resource.

If you are open, curious, and hungry to learn about how you can build and leverage relationships in authentic and genuine ways, this book is for you. You'll discover the latest research on the role of relationships in advancing careers; you'll be treated to the wisdom Rosina has gained from her own career and the collective experience of WUI, and you'll walk in the shoes of some amazing leaders, both female and male.

Time is wasting . . . Start reading!

Dr. Sheila A. Robinson
Founder, Publisher, and CEO
Diversity Woman Media

CHAPTER 1

MY WORK WASN'T SPEAKING FOR ME

To be happy, I've discovered, you've got to run toward
something: meaningful work; a hopeful, inspiring vision
of your future; and good relationships with the people you
work with every day.
— Annie McKee

A single piece of feedback transformed my view of how
others were seeing me. It also showed me what others
needed from me to understand my value to the organization
where I worked. I was lucky to get this pivotal piece of feedback early in my career. Actually, I was lucky to get this piece
of feedback at all—because women rarely get the feedback
they need to understand the mysteries of how organizations
work.

The setting was a manufacturing plant where I was head of
human resources. I was 30 years old and navigating my first
position as a member of a management team. I was the only
woman on the team.

As you can imagine, I was working hard to prove my value to all the other team members. I wanted to make sure that I
not only performed well in every task but also surpassed everyone's expectations. I had high expectations of myself and

expected that others did as well. As far as I could tell, every-thing was going well.

One day, I was walking through the plant with our head of engineering, Don, whose 6'4" frame towered over me. We were talking about a variety of issues when Don suddenly stopped and said, "Do you know what your problem is, Rosina?"

Startled and barely managing to suppress the offense I felt, I answered, "No, Don. What's my problem?" I wasn't aware of any problem. In the absence of criticism, I assumed I was per-forming well and had the same respect as everyone else on the management team.

Don said, "Everyone thinks he can do your job."

I was taken aback, but I also immediately realized that Don was telling me something important. I had been working under the assumption that people saw my work and understood that I was adding value to the business. I thought my work spoke for itself—that I didn't need to add words or promote myself to prove my worth.

I had failed to realize that as I sat around the table at man-agement meetings, if I didn't talk about my knowledge of the business and explain the business context around the work I was doing, other team members had no way to know that I un-derstood the business, let alone was adding value.

Don's feedback gave me such a moment of clarity that I simply stopped and said, "Thank you."

From that point on, I consistently thought about framing my work and recommendations in the context of their impact on the business. I asked myself what the plant manager needed to know so that he could tap into me more, leverage me, and make sure we were aligned around various issues. I started approaching everything I did and every person I needed to in-fluence in an entirely different way.

Today, as President and Chief Executive Officer of WOMEN Unlimited, Inc. (WUI), I oversee a team whose initiatives help major corporations pinpoint, develop, and retain their diverse leadership talent. WUI is the go-to development partner for over 200 leading organizations.

Our three-prong development approach, which includes mentoring, education, and networking, is much more than a seminar or quick-fix approach. Because women may be in our programs for up to a year, we get to know them, their strengths, frustrations, and patterns.

One of the most common frustrations we hear from intelligent and competent women who have been employed by the same corporation for a while is that their work is not speaking for itself—and it should. In other words, these women are doing great things, but nobody seems to be noticing or promoting them because of that great work. In response, these women often consider looking outside the company for another opportunity.

The women who enter our programs, particularly those at mid-career level, are typically fiercely independent—and they consider this an asset. They want to stay removed from office politics and hate the idea of "playing the game" to get ahead. While these women want to grow their careers and move into more significant leadership positions, they aren't willing to do so at the expense of their authenticity.

For these women, WUI strives to be the voice of Don, the engineering manager who gave me the gift of feedback. We try to help our participants understand that the misalignment between them and their organization is based, at least in part, on faulty assumptions. Fierce independence, a trait that can help an individual contributor get her work done, can also leave a person isolated and uninformed about the organization as a whole. Such independence, by definition, also leaves the organization uninformed about that individual's talents and contributions, a kiss of death for a woman who wants a promotion.

While office politics suggests an ugly dynamic, all organizations, even little league sports, need rules and scorekeepers to function. It doesn't automatically taint a person to understand the rules and make choices within them.

Some women are so quick to take a stand against inauthenticity that they inadvertently resist change and growth. While we should only be ourselves, we can't expect to effectively lead others if we are failing to grow and evolve. In today's complex business world, rigidity is a kiss of death, and adaptability is a key leadership skill.

So, how do successful women leaders navigate these tricky waters? How do they understand their work, their colleagues, and their organizations? How do they get others to notice their work and contributions without being braggarts? How do they win at the game without being sullied by it? How do they get a seat at the table and then get others at the table to respect and promote their ideas and perspectives?

Our work at WUI is all about finding and sharing the answers to these questions. We collaborate with and learn from the best experts and researchers in the field of leadership. We provide workshops and mentors (both male and female) to help our participants answer the questions for themselves and then apply those answers to their careers. We also work with our participants' managers, who gain insight and understanding on what they need to do to support and develop the women on their teams. Managers learn to support women with specific behaviors rather than the generalities they might encounter in quick-fix programs.

We consistently find that one of the most important ingredients for leadership growth and advancement is strong and diverse relationships. In the research I completed for my doctorate, I discovered that having access to a mentor doesn't guarantee growth or promotion. Mentor-mentee relationships work only when the mentee is *intentional* about building and leveraging the relationship.

What's more, I've learned that lack of a formal mentor relationship doesn't necessarily limit a woman's potential for advancement. No single relationship is the ticket to promotion. Successful leaders are intentional about building relationships with multiple people and groups, including executives, peers, internal and external business partners, and industry groups. Some of these relationships may be formalized and enduring. Others may involve a single conversation in which a woman asks a senior manager for feedback on a specific presentation.

Successful women are strategic about interactions with their mentors and others, formulating clear goals so that the relationships can support their specific aims and ambitions. Savvy women also apply the insights they gain from others so they can "show up" in new ways that advance their growth and development. Further, they invest in building relationships with key people inside and outside the organization. This allows them to get a bigger picture of the business and how things fit within the organization and industry. It also provides the pathway to discover any gaps between how they desire to be seen as a professional and how others see them.

My goal for this book is to take my research and the work of WUI on relationships further and deeper. To supplement what I've learned in the research and our experience with thousands of women, I interviewed 10 strong leaders, ranging from seasoned executives to up-and-coming leaders. I wanted to learn how these leaders, both women and men, think about building relationships and how they leveraged their relationships throughout their careers. I asked them to tell me about the role of relationships in their career progression. I invited these leaders to tell their stories and to share the practical strategies that have worked for them. You can read about these leaders and my relationships with them immediately following this chapter.

The results are rich, diverse, and profoundly hopeful. Of course, the barriers women face in advancing in today's organization are complex and well documented. There are cultural, organizational, and managerial issues as well as barriers that women create for themselves. There are layers upon layers to the problem, and we can become easily discouraged.

In writing this book, I'm focusing on a significant element women *can* control. Women have the power to build relationships and leverage those relationships for bigger ways to contribute and grow their careers. If you are interested in standing up to take control of your own career, this book is for you. You'll discover research findings, tools, and stories all working together to provide what you need to shape your own future.

PROFILE OF SUCCESS

As I interviewed strong leaders for this book and considered others I know from WUI and my own career, a profile of a strong leader emerged. Listening to diverse stories, varied career paths, and perspectives about relationships, I noticed a pattern of attributes in exceptional leaders. I've come to think of these attributes as a mindset that permeates everything successful leaders do, including the building and growing of relationships.

I now believe that to talk about techniques for building and leveraging relationships without discussing mindset would be a disservice to you. The six attributes or characteristics that interact in fluid ways in the leaders we identified as strong and successful leadership role models are as follows:

1. Value Relationships
2. Intentionality
3. Curiosity
4. Self-Awareness
5. Purpose and Passion
6. Realism

1. VALUE RELATIONSHIPS

Strong leaders, if they hadn't known it from the beginning, come to a point when they realize that fierce independence is a liability rather than an asset. They seek relationships of all kinds, with peers, managers, executives, professionals outside of the organization, and more. This is not because these leaders feel less than competent; it is because they know that any one person or unit has limited insight—especially in today's complex and fast-changing environments.

2. INTENTIONALITY

The individuals I interviewed have a clear understanding that they alone are responsible for their own careers. Rather than wait around for a manager or human resource professional to notice and take an interest in their careers, these individuals are intentional about where they want to go, and the strategies needed to get there. They figure out where they can best contribute to an industry and organization and chart a path to get there.

3. CURIOSITY

In interview after interview, leaders explained how they want to learn everything they can—about the business, their clients, team members, counterparts, the organization's executives, and more. These individuals have a high strong desire to know how pieces fit together to make a whole, and how what they and their team members do fits into the whole.

This curiosity extends beyond the confines of the office. Strong leaders have a pure joy in learning and exploring. They seek out diverse perspectives and learning experiences with a broad brush, gathering insights from professional, community, and family connections as well as from connections at work. I'd go so far as to say these leaders find the process of discovering new perspectives invigorating. If you doubt the importance of this trait, consider these words attributed to a female leader who certainly left her mark upon the world, Eleanor Roosevelt: "I think, at a child's birth, if a mother could ask a fairy godmother to endow it with the most useful gift, that gift would be curiosity."

When contemplating a career change or other big step, leaders who habitually ask questions and seek to understand people, processes, and points of view already have access to divergent perspectives and insights to inform their thinking and decision-making. All this information is invaluable as they move up the organizational ladder and must work with others who have conflicting priorities. Those who know and appreciate other points of view have an edge when navigating ambiguous situations. Leaders with an expansive mindset are open to possibilities, even ideas they might never have thought of themselves.

4.   SELF-AWARENESS

Curiosity about others, of course, has limited value for individuals who aren't curious about themselves and how others see them. The leaders I interviewed seek to know how others perceive them and to identify gaps between this and how they want to be seen. They put effort into growing their self-awareness as well as their skill set. This requires a willingness to receive feedback, even when that feedback is difficult to hear. It requires a commitment to put aside defensiveness and evaluate feedback as objectively as possible. In other words, it requires courage and a willingness to change.

Rather than just take information in, strong leaders make time to think, process, and integrate information. They are attentive to new trends and think about what those trends might mean for their business.

5. PURPOSE AND PASSION

In addition to curiosity and the need for self-awareness, strong leaders are driven by purpose and a passion to contribute. The leaders I interviewed deliberately invested time and thought into discovering their talents and figuring out what career and position was right for them in terms of making the biggest possible contribution. They worked hard to obtain the best-fit position, and once they got to that spot, they experienced the joy of making a difference. They consider it a leadership duty to help their team members find this same type of joy.

6. REALISM

Strong leaders have their heads up rather than down. They identify the scorekeepers in their organizations, and they work to influence them. They uncover the formal and informal rules of their organizations, and they work within them in intentional ways. If they break a rule, they do so deliberately, having considered the consequences.

Women entering our programs express deep concerns about compromising their authenticity by playing the game. For the strong leaders I interviewed, integrity and authenticity are givens, foundational—but they understand authenticity differently than the women entering our programs do. The interviewees agree that authenticity is dynamic rather than static, something that changes as a person grows and changes roles. It has some resemblance to how people change hairstyles and clothing as they mature. Strong leaders don't change who they are, but they show up in ways appropriate to their position. At the same time, they know their boundaries. If asked to show up in a way that violates their values, strong leaders take a stand.

WHAT TO EXPECT IN THE PAGES THAT FOLLOW

After relating the inspirational story of WUI's founder, Jean Otte, Chapter 2 explores why building a strong network is essential for every aspiring leader's career. You'll discover seven compelling reasons why everyone who wants to grow a career needs a strong network. You'll complete this chapter with a new appreciation for the value of a network for you. You won't be wondering if building a network is worth the effort; you'll just be eager to get started.

Chapter 3 makes the case that building a successful network begins with a mindset—one that understands that mentors are all around us. They are the people who can help us explore different perspectives, answer our questions, act as sounding boards, and share their wisdom with us. Drawing on the work of Kathy Kram and other researchers, as well as stories from my interviewees, this chapter digs deep into what's involved in building a developmental network.

Chapter 4 will guide you to think strategically about your network, beginning by making a map of your current relationships. Steps include evaluating your attitude, assessing your current performance, setting deliberate goals, initiating conversations, and more. Stories from successful leaders reveal strategies that have worked across a variety of situations and industries. These strategies are surprisingly manageable and nonthreatening, even when approaching senior leaders.

Without feedback, you can't know whether or not your actions and performance are effective. But knowing that feedback is essential to growth and performance doesn't lessen the natural fears we have of being criticized. In Chapter 5, interviewees share their stories and strategies for responding to feedback in productive ways. They share the belief that feedback is neutral data that needs to be evaluated—but it's also a gift that needs to be appreciated.

With the title "If Relationships and Visibility Are So Important to Career Growth, Why Do Women Hide?", Chapter 6 explores the reasons behind many women's failure to make their contributions at work known. Why do so many women hunker down and expect their work to shine on its own? Like other chapters, this one looks to research as well as the experiences and stories employed by interviewees to dig deep.

The women who enter WUI programs tend to be risk-averse, like most women. But leaders who make it to the top of their organizations do so by taking ownership of their careers and embracing strategic risks. Owning your career means strategically building your core skills, expanding your responsibilities, and expanding your network both inside and outside your organization. For some people, this happens during a natural career progression in one organization. For others, it happens through volunteering for assignments outside their daily job opportunities. For others, it requires changing companies. Chapter 7 describes the diverse stories of how my interviewees have successfully embraced risk. You'll be glad to know that there are an endless number of ways to chart your own path forward.

Successful performance at high levels of organizations is impossible without deliberate strategy. Yet, even the phrase playing the game leaves a nasty taste in the mouths of many women. Most of us have a deep commitment to authenticity and fear that playing the game will compromise us. Chapter 8 explores how successful leaders navigate the ambiguous situations that come with the diverse priorities and perspectives faced in senior management positions. Research and stories reveal how to build and leverage a network to handle such situations without compromising integrity.

Among the shifts needed for success in a senior role in an organization is the shift in self-perception from one who performs to one who creates capacity in others to perform. This work involves mentoring others, helping them take calculated risks, giving performance feedback, and sponsoring them for job changes that provide learning and growth experiences. Chapter 9 provides advice and examples of how to do this effectively.

Once we get to Chapter 10, we'll have come full circle. I trust you'll have new perspectives, new role models, some surprisingly manageable strategies, and a boatload of inspiration. You'll be ready to take action in new ways.

STRONG LEADERS YOU'LL MEET IN THESE PAGES

The following 10 leaders graciously agreed to be interviewed and share their insights for this book. I admire each of them and am grateful for their participation. You'll notice that some of these leaders have mentored for and/or participated in WUI programs. Our programs include the following:

IMPOWER

Impower prepares early-career women to contribute to corporate goals and objectives. This six-month program focuses on ways for women to "own" their careers, develop smart relationships, build confidence, bolster their organization-wide impact, and espouse change and innovation.

LEAD

The LEAD program is for high-potential women with a minimum of seven years of managerial experience. The program focuses on developing strategic alliances, thinking globally, learning successful risk-taking strategies, and managing change. The program includes 12 sessions, on-the-job assignments, one-on-one and team mentoring by leading corporate executives, an individual development planning process, and networking and team-building exercises.

THE FEW

The FEW is a by-invitation only executive leadership program that helps senior women increase their contributions to corporate success while fine-tuning their high-level executive skills.

COURTNEY COLLINS

Courtney is the Senior Director of Customer Experience Centers for AppDynamics, a Cisco Company. With over 15 years of creative and technical experience, she leads teams in designing and delivering world-class customer experiences and executive engagements. As a certified Design Thinking Facilitator, Courtney drives customer co-creation for AppDynamics' and Cisco's top-tier customers. Most of all, she relishes the magic of creating memorable and meaningful experiences—not just for customers, but also for everyone at work and at home.

> Courtney graduated from the San Francisco WOMEN Unlimited LEAD program in May 2016. She was recognized by her peers as a Future Leader to Watch. Courtney has mentored for both LEAD and IMpower, and one of her direct reports is currently thriving in the LEAD program.

AMY GONZALES

Amy is Vice President of Global Learning and Development for WUI. Amy held senior and line management positions in high technology and service industries, where she first developed her

appetite for creating powerful learning strategies for global audi-
ences. Amy's work with WUI and in her consulting practice
focuses on executive presence, leadership effectiveness, and
communication. Her key focus is to challenge leaders at all
levels to move beyond their limits to achieve greater success.

> Amy was one of the "originals" working with Jean Otte as
> she launched WUI. She started the programs in California
> in 1996, overseeing the West Coast Programs until she
> joined WUI's management team in 2014. Amy's ability to
> create a safe and fun learning environment has been key
> to her success.

ANN CALELLO GROCCIA

Ann is Vice President of Corporate Partner Relationships for
WUI. She spent 20 years at Fidelity Investments, where she
exceled in leadership roles as Executive Vice President of Relationship Management and Implementation for the Broker
Dealer marketplace. Ann's diverse business experience, combined with her executive coaching and consulting expertise,
support her passion for working with business leaders and their
teams.

> When Ann joined WUI, she oversaw the Boston-area
> programs. Her passion for developing relationships con-
> tributes to her success. She joined WUI's management
> team in 2014.

TONY HUNTER

Tony is known for his success as an architect of change and a
leader of business transformation. His approach to leadership
was developed over a 20-year career at Tribune Publishing.
He refined his approach to transforming organizations during
a period of radical change and digital disruption. As CEO of
Tribune Publishing, Tony's leadership led to improved em-

ployee engagement and exceptional business results. He is the former chair of the News Media Alliance, Chair Emeritus of Metropolitan Family Services, and a United Way board member. Tony is currently Chairman of Revolution Enterprises, an Illinois-based cannabis company.

> Tony has sponsored women in our programs since we launched programs in Chicago in 1995. A strong leader, he also participated as mentor and panelist and encouraged many of his senior leaders to be mentors.

KATHY E. KRAM, PHD

Kathy is the R. C. Shipley Professor in Management, Emerita, at Boston University. Her primary interests are in the areas of leadership development, relational learning, mentoring, coaching and developmental networks, and change processes in organizations. Her book, *Mentoring at Work*, has been cited in a wide range of journals. Dr. Kram consults with a variety of organizations that want to enhance their leadership development practices using mentoring, mentoring circles, and peer coaching.

Dr. Kram has co-authored several books, including *Strategic Relationships at Work: Creating Your Circle of Mentors, Sponsors, and Peers for Success in Business and Life* (with Dr. Belle Rose Ragins) and *Peer Coaching at Work: Principles and Practices* (with Drs. Polly Parker, Douglas (Tim) Hall and Ilene Wasserman).

> When I was completing the research for my dissertation, I reached out to Dr. Kram, a thought leader in mentoring. I found her to be very generous with her time as she shared her knowledge. She not only researches developmental relationships, but she also lives them!

SANDRA BEACH LIN

Sandy is a member of the boards of directors of American Electric Power, PolyOne Corporation, Trinseo, and Interface Biologics. She is the retired President and Chief Executive Officer of Calisolar, Inc. (now Silicor Materials). Sandy previously served as Corporate Executive Vice President of Celanese Corporation. Prior to Celanese, she held senior executive positions at Avery Dennison Corporation, Alcoa, and Honeywell International. In 2013, she was named to the National Association of Corporate Directors (NACD) Directorship 100. She is a member of the Committee of 200, the International Women's Forum, the Dallas Assembly, and is a founding member of Paradigm for Parity®.

> Sandy was introduced to WUI when she participated as a mentor. She later participated in The FEW and was also a member of WUI President's Advisory Council.

JENNIFER MCCORMICK

Jennifer enjoyed a robust career in manufacturing and sales in the apparel industry and consumer packaged goods. She had a long tenure at Levi Strauss & Co. where she directed the largest distribution center, oversaw the new CASI facility construction distribution facility, and led a team of sales professionals for Levi's® Brand for men's and boys' business.

Jennifer expanded her career by moving to Morton Salt as Senior Director of Customer Service and Execution. She has also held roles leading the B2B Industrial Sales Team for North America and the Consumer Marketing and Sales Planning Organization. Jennifer is currently Vice President of Operations for the Americas, overseeing 26 locations and 2,600 employees. She is active in industry user groups, promoting continuous education and professional networking.

I met Jennifer when she participated as a mentor in the
Chicago LEAD program and got to know her when she
participated in The FEW. She was also a member of WUI
President's Advisory Council.

Annie McKee, PhD

Annie is a best-selling author, respected academic, speaker,
and advisor to top global leaders. Annie is also a senior Fellow
at the University of Pennsylvania Graduate School of Education, where she teaches and leads the PennCLO Executive Doctoral Program. Annie uses a person-centered approach to help
leaders develop their emotional intelligence and enhance their
strategic thinking about how each one of us can create better
and more compassionate workplaces. Annie's books include
*How to Be Happy at Work: The Power of Purpose, Hope, and
Friendship; Primal Leadership* (with Daniel Goleman and
Richard Boyatzis)*;* and *Resonant Leadership* (with Richard
Boyatzis).

I met Annie when she came to the University of Pennsylvania to oversee the PennCLO Program. She provided
great support to me as I completed my dissertation and
continues to be a great friend and mentor.

Susan Sobbott

Susan is a board member, advisor, speaker, and avid student of
new business opportunities, following a 28-year distinguished
career at American Express, where she was President of Global
Commercial Services. When Susan was President and General
Manager of OPEN Small Business, she spearheaded the crea-
tion of "Small Business Saturday." Susan currently serves on
the boards of The Children's Place and Red Ventures. She is an
avid supporter of women entrepreneurs and has been recog-

nized for her work advocating for women's leadership and advancing the prosperity of business customers.

> I met Susan when she participated as a mentor for WUI. When she later participated in The FEW, Susan developed a strong relationship with Jean Otte, who continued as Susan's mentor long after the program ended.

JENNIFER WILLIAMS

Jennifer is a Strategic Project Manager for the Voice of Customer Individual Solutions Group—Customer Experience, at Prudential Financial, Inc. She has over 10 years of experience in financial services, project management, insurance, and customer experience.

Managing people and projects on a global scale, Jenny understands how important relationships and networking can be to get the job done.

> A graduate of WUI Boston WUI LEAD program, Jenny was recognized by her peers for successfully exemplifying all three pillars of the program. Since graduation, Jenny mentors for IMpower.

JOHN (JACK) L. YURISH

Jack is President of J.L. Yurish Associates, Inc. and Co-founder and Principal of the Cambridge Management Institute. With over 50 years of management and consulting experience, he has worked with firms such as Western Electric, ITT, the Hertz Corporation, and The American Management Association. Jack's last corporate position, the result of participating in a leveraged buyout, was Executive Vice President and an owner of National Car Rental Systems, Inc.

Jack met Jean M. Otte at National Car Rental Systems and became her mentor. When Jean launched WUI in 1994, Jack continued to provide support and mentorship. He continues to serve as a board member for WUI.

> Jack and I met when Jean launched WUI. Jean hosted a meeting of corporate partners to gain feedback on the program. Jack noticed my contributions and suggested to Jean that she "keep an eye" on me. A few years later, I joined WUI.

CHAPTER 2

SEVEN REASONS
YOU NEED A NETWORK

*Living without feedback is like trying to drive a car with
no dashboard or performance indicators (gas, oil, water
level, etc.). Without feedback, you can't know whether
your actions and performance are effective or not.*

— Jack Yurish

Chances are, WUI's beloved founder and chief role model,
Jean Otte, had her share of fears. Fear of standing up for
herself and asking for help weren't among them. Because Jean
was a beloved mentor and friend, I'll tell her story in a personal
way, using her first name, as I did in the WUI offices before
Jean passed away in 2018.

In 1987, Jean was head of customer service at National
Car Rental Systems when new owners arrived. A colleague
advised Jean not to say much when she went into her first
meeting with the "five white guys" who were then in charge.

Jean categorically rejected this advice. In fact, she went into the meeting with charts explaining why she should get a
raise and a promotion. Jean made the case that she was one of

the most important people in the company—because she and her team members were the ones talking to customers daily.

Jean caught the attention of Jack Yurish, who, as one of the five white guys, was an executive vice president and an owner of the company. Yurish mentored Jean, helping her to understand the most effective ways to present her ideas in that organizational climate. Yurish became Jean's sponsor, and the two enjoyed a long and supportive friendship.

Eventually, Jean became a corporate vice president at National, with added responsibility for training and quality. A tireless mentor and sponsor herself, Jean left National in 1993 with the intention of setting up her own company, WOMEN Unlimited, Inc., to develop female leaders to advance their careers. To date, more than 13,000 women have completed programs at WUI.

From today's vantage point, it's clear that Jean had the right "stuff" to launch a successful business. But what were her secret ingredients? How did she do it?

By the time Jean was ready to act on her plan for WUI, she had already developed an extensive network. For example, Jean was president of SOCAP International, a collaborative community of best-in-class customer care experts across all industries. Members include vice presidents, directors, managers, and specialists, many of whom come from some of the world's most recognized Fortune 1000 companies. Executives at startup and emerging companies are also members.

You can imagine the number of professional friendships Jean formed in the many years of serving this association until she was ultimately chosen to be president. Giving, mentoring, and serving were daily activities for Jean, both inside and outside of her official workplace. Although Jean passed away in 2018, her relational mindset of friendship, support, and service still permeates the organization she founded. Personally and professionally, I owe so much to Jean.

When she arrived in New York from Minnesota to launch WUI, Jean reached out to her network to discuss her vision. And she asked the individuals in her network to introduce her to other leaders. It worked.

For example, through SOCAP, Jean met Grace Richardson, a senior leader at Colgate. Richardson introduced Jean to Michelle Mays, who immediately saw the value in Jean's vision. Colgate became WUI's first corporate partner.

I'm not suggesting the process of establishing and growing WUI was easy. It took passion, perseverance, and a well-honed pitch. I recall Jean sharing that one of her former bosses told her she was foolish to try to launch a program in New York, as it was difficult to start a business there. Here's the kicker: he said it would be especially hard for a woman! In trying to dissuade Jean, this former boss simply fueled her passion.

Finally, on April 18, 1994, without brochures or fancy marketing materials, Jean launched the first WUI program in New York. She had hoped to have 50 women in that first class, but she settled for fewer than 20. Among the companies represented were Colgate, Elizabeth Arden, Washington Mutual, Volvo Cars of North America, and Moody's Investor Service.

After Jean launched the first program, she reached out to the companies that had sponsored women in the program, including the participants' managers and mentors, to get feedback. Jean displayed remarkable openness and curiosity in her quest to learn which elements of the program and partnership people found valuable. She was equally interested in understanding the areas in which the program could improve. Because she was able to gather this information without being defensive, Jean was able to grow the programs, ensuring they met the needs of women and organizations at that time and were ready for the future. We still actively seek feedback from our participants and corporate partners today and believe it is one of the reasons we remain relevant.

As Jean was meeting with various companies, she came to Degussa, where I worked at the time. Jack Yurish had introduced Jean to Degussa's chief human resource officer, Ed Sims. He introduced me to Jean, who shared her vision with me. I was a bit resistant at first, but Jean's vision and enthusiasm piqued my interest.

We enrolled some women in the program as a pilot, and Jean asked me to serve as a mentor. After the program was completed, Jean invited me to attend a meeting to provide her with feedback on our experience. Thus began a professional relationship that evolved into a personal friendship.

Several years later when I left Degussa and started consulting, I continued to mentor for WUI and stayed in contact with Jean. Not long after, Jean asked me to join WUI. Having built the company, she needed someone to help her in the Northeast. This afforded me the opportunity to focus on two things I love doing: helping women find their career joy *and* helping grow a business.

Meanwhile, Amy Gonzales, who had been mentored by Jean at National Car Rental, was still in touch with Jean. Gonzales was working in training and development, management development, and executive development in a high-tech organization. When Gonzales heard about Jean's plan, she fell in love with the mission and the opportunity to make an impact. She began working with WUI on the side. Two years later, Gonzales told Jean that the organization needed a West Coast representative—and that she should be that person.

Gonzales recalls some of the early years of WUI. She says, "Jean would call and ask us (a few close professional friends) to help and say, 'I can't pay you.'"

We would respond, "Sure, it sounds great."

Jean would continue, "And you have to stay in my apartment and sleep on the couch because I can't afford a hotel, but this is going to be good. I'll make you a home-cooked meal."

Jean had a high degree of relationship capital, and she leveraged that capital for success. Her story illustrates the power of building and leveraging relationships, and it matches current research that claims relationship capital is essential to success.

Following in Jean's footsteps, we encourage the women in our programs to think about developmental relationships in broad terms. The hope that one person will meet all a woman's (or man's) needs for guidance, exposure, and opportunities is ineffective as a strategy. In the complex world in which we work, no one person can provide everything needed to successfully navigate a career. No one has access to the sum of technical knowledge, political know-how, global dynamics, and developmental guidance a growing leader needs.

Even if I can convince you that building a broad network is important, you might still push back. You might say I'm presenting an unfair example—that Jean is an example of a special person, gifted with confidence and hutzpah few others possess. You might explain that you are an introvert and the idea of putting yourself out there makes you a nervous wreck. You might complain about time limitations, your workload, or the feeling of inauthenticity you have when making small talk at artificially contrived gatherings. In short, you might respond with the resistance common to women.

Professor of Organizational Behavior at London Business School, Herminia Ibarra, asked a group of men and women to list all the contacts they consult for matters of work and the friends they socialize with outside of work. The answers revealed a distinct difference in how men and women handle relationships. In a 2018 *Wall Street Journal* article, Ibarra explains,

> Men often have some people on both lists—they'll play squash or go to dinner with some of those work contacts. Women, in contrast, are more likely to have two separate lists. This difference is most pronounced for women who have children, when outside-of-work relationships tend to become more driven by school activities and family. All of which means it takes longer for women to achieve influence.

It's hard to disagree with Ibarra's logical conclusion:

> [This] increases the likelihood that women will have unfavorable views about networking. The more we differ from key stakeholders, and the more we have to go out of our way to interact informally with them, the more likely we'll view networking as disingenuous and calculating. So, women begin to see networking as being about selfish gain and using people.

When you feel disingenuous and calculating about an activity, you are naturally prone to avoid that activity. We see ample evidence of this discomfort and avoidance in the participants, especially those at mid-career level, entering our programs.

Unfortunately, this natural avoidance reaction often serves as career self-sabotage. The most successful leaders, women and men, are intentional about building and leveraging relationships throughout their careers. They are acutely aware of the *essential need* for relationships, and they also tend to have a *broader definition* of networking and relationship-building than others do.

Let's begin by looking at seven reasons we all need relationships to be successful in our careers. At this point, I'll
loosely refer to these as mentoring relationships.

1. Narrow the perception gap

2. Move forward with support

3. Gain advocates at all levels

4. Acquire technical and business knowledge

5. Think critically

6. Experience mutual discovery and joy

7. Navigate the ambiguity that comes with career growth

1. NARROW THE PERCEPTION GAP

According to Margarita Mayo, in a *Harvard Business Review*
article called "The Gender Gap in Feedback and Self-
Perception," research clearly indicates that all of us, male and
female, are prone to overestimate our own performance. Without feedback from others, a perception gap exists, preventing
us from making changes that could improve our performance
and likelihood for promotion. I know this firsthand, because it
happened to me.

Well into my career, I had become part of the management
team in a large multinational chemical company. I was promoted from overseeing plant operations to a corporate headquarters
role. It was thrilling to be getting a seat at the table.

In the years before I received this promotion, I had participated in several 360-degree assessments that highlighted my
areas of strength as well as areas needing development. I consistently received feedback on the need to soften my forceful
communication style.

Dismissing the feedback, I decided those who provided it
were ill-informed. I knew I was direct, but this was a natural

style that got results. Having been brought up in a large Italian family, I was taught to speak in a direct fashion. This style was reinforced by my years working in manufacturing plants.

Then, as part of my development in my new headquarters job, I attended a leadership program with my colleagues. In the context of a group exercise, a colleague shared, "I enjoy working with you, Rosina, but I don't think I would follow you out of the foxhole."

Taken aback, I drew in a quick breath. Suddenly, all the 360 feedback I had received through the years came flooding back. The feedback my new colleague shared helped me understand that my communication style made people feel I was dragging them up the hill with me. My forceful style, combined with poor listening skills, was creating a barrier to my effectiveness and success.

This incident represents a second instance of luck in my professional growth—the first having been Don, the engineer who told me that all my colleagues thought they could do my HR job. In both cases, a colleague's willingness to provide honest feedback helped me understand the gap between my self-perception and how others perceived me.

I am making it sound like accepting this feedback was an easy process—but it was not. It took work to make my way through my defensiveness and my internal justifications. In the end, since I wanted to be effective, I needed to accept and then use this insight to evolve my skills.

2. MOVE FORWARD WITH SUPPORT

Senior Fellow at the University of Pennsylvania Graduate School of Education and advisor to top global leaders, Annie McKee has a career story that is anything but typical. Rather than go to college at 18, McKee married very young, had kids, and found herself living in abject poverty for many years. Her first mentor was Mary Burton, a woman for whom McKee cleaned house. Gently, and with a great deal of respect, Burton occasionally reminded McKee that she was smart, confident, and able to do more than clean houses and wait tables. Because of how the advice was given—in the context of dignity and valuing the contribution she was making—McKee was able to receive this feedback and maintain a lifelong friendship with Burton.

Roughly eight years later, McKee was mother to a 6-month-old and a 3-year-old, living in poverty in rural Hawaii. She had a husband who seemed comfortable with their lifestyle, as difficult as it was to rely on welfare and public assistance. A doctor encouraged her to make a visit to someone named Sister Anna. Reluctant and desperate, McKee got on her bike with her two babies and went to meet this nun. She discovered a group of women in a ramshackle Quonset hut, all busily working on a variety of women's issues that touched each of them personally—education for their children, ensuring there was enough food at the end of the month, and helping women build the confidence to step away from abusive relationships.

For eight years, McKee belonged to this busy group. They created soup kitchens for themselves and others; they infiltrated the public school system to teach classes on harmony and dealing with violence and drugs; and they took global political action.

Sister Anna and these women became an incredible source of support to McKee, just as she became to them. Then, somewhere along the way, McKee realized that without education, she would never be able to feed her family or have the life she dreamed of, even with the wonderful help of the women's support group.

McKee decided to enroll in community college, but she was terrified. Knowing this would be the case, the group sent one woman, Rhonda, to stand next to McKee in line to register to make sure she wouldn't leave. Rhonda stood next to her saying, "You're not going to leave. I started here last semester; I'm taking one class. You are not going to leave."

McKee did not leave. Even after giving birth to her third child, she continued her studies. She quickly found her way from community college to a four-year college, and then to graduate school and an illustrious career as a professor and best-selling author. She says,

> The support of the women behind me and around me got me there and got me through. And I got them through. Each of the women ended up going to college, which was unheard of in that neighborhood, because they had no money, and little confidence.

3.   GAIN ADVOCATES AT ALL LEVELS

When we talk about leveraging relationships, many people automatically think about connecting with a key executive who can sponsor them. But unless it occurs organically, sponsorship can be hard to come by, and it's only one part of the successful relationship equation.

Typically, sponsorship is earned rather than requested or appointed. It typically begins when a senior person has the opportunity to see demonstrated work and potential—and takes interest. Jack Yurish noticed that Jean was a go-to person at National Car Rental Systems when he arrived as an executive there. Yurish championed Jean's ideas, but only after she did the background work to prove those ideas. Subsequently, their relationship evolved in many ways.

Richard Boyatzis, a recognized expert in the field of emotional intelligence, behavior change, and competence, was a professor at Case Western Reserve University when Annie McKee was in graduate school there. Boyatzis recognized McKee's potential and became a sponsor. The two became co-authors with Daniel Goleman. Eventually, the relationship evolved and Boyatzis and McKee became peers.

But again, sponsorship is only one piece of the successful relationship puzzle. Long before Susan Sobbott took on the role of president for American Express Global Commercial Services, she had her first day at the company. On that day, Sobbott had a fluke opportunity to participate in a small-group lunch with two senior executives. One of the executives said something Sobbott took to heart and frequently shares with others. He said,

> The people who will be most important to you in your career are your peers. They are far more important than the people above you. You want to make sure you have a very strong relationship with your peers. When somebody's looking to hire you, they are the ones who will be asked about you.

4.   ACQUIRE TECHNICAL AND BUSINESS KNOWLEDGE

Doing any job well requires knowledge. We not only need to acquire knowledge that pertains to our technical department or niche, we need to know how various segments of the business work together, and how the organization makes money and keeps score. Typically, we come by this knowledge through relationships.

For example, in all my jobs, I made it a practice to get to know the controller, the one who understood the numbers and how each department contributed. Good sales representatives seek out relationships with individuals who understand the technical aspects of their products. Demonstrating interest by requesting interviews and asking questions with sincere interest not only helps you to fill out your knowledge base, but it also makes you likeable and memorable to others.

Leaders who are strategic about their careers often raise their hands to participate on cross-departmental projects. Working on project-based tasks with others allows you to learn their priorities and perspectives while building relationships and demonstrating your own competence and work ethic.

5.   THINK CRITICALLY

Strong leaders know that their knowledge and perceptions, however educated and insightful they might be, are incomplete. All humans are limited by their backgrounds and biases, especially the ones of which they are unaware. Strong leaders intentionally build relationships with people to have access to divergent points of view—in assessing ambiguous situations, difficult conversations, and career moves.

For example, Vice President of Operations for Morton Salt, Jennifer McCormick, describes herself as a recovering worrier who learned that feedback could ease her internal struggles and help her to think critically. She explains how she leveraged her relationship with a boss to sharpen her thinking while reducing worries about making wrong decisions.

> I got to the point where I was not sleeping well and felt frustrated with myself over it. I finally just made the connection that, "You know what, Jen? You are in control here. You're not in control of everything in your life, but you are absolutely in control of managing the things that you're worried about, getting answers to the questions that you have in your head, and figuring out how to deal with them."

So, it started, quite frankly, with my boss. I decided that I just needed to ask for feedback. In some cases, I had a new role or was presented with a new challenge. I thought I knew what to do but I wasn't completely confident and sure. I'd work up the courage to say, "Here's the problem. Here's what I think I need to do. Can you give me feedback on how that sounds?" And we'd work through the problem together.

Analyzing ideas with the help of mentors, managers, and colleagues helps you to think objectively. Sometimes the other person merely needs to offer you good questions. At other times, the person may guide you through a thinking process. For example, Jack Yurish, who has over 50 years of management and consulting experience, makes a point of emphasizing a focus on results versus activities. In any given situation, he encourages associates to consider a structured analysis of the performance, people, and processes involved.

6.   EXPERIENCE MUTUAL DISCOVERY AND JOY

My highest purpose as a professional is to help others discover joy in their careers. That's why it was particularly gratifying to me when people I interviewed said they built relationships to enjoy discovering different perspectives. Sandy Beach Lin simply said, "I have a high degree of curiosity. I like meeting people and learning from them."

As a retired executive who sits on multiple boards, Lin is at the point in her career where she seeks relationships in which she can learn and enjoy the views of another person. And Annie McKee, also at a mature point in her career, explained that relationships work when there is a mutual desire to get to know one another. This is as true of mentor/mentee relationships as it is of peer relationships. Relationships not only help us meet our career goals, but they also enrich our lives. Who doesn't need to make time for that?

As you can see from the examples in this chapter, when I think of networking, building, and leveraging relationships, I'm defining those words with a broad brush. When I talk about networking, I'm not talking about events in which you balance appetizers on small plates while engaging in awkward small talk, hoping to be remembered. I'm talking about building meaningful relationships as an essential piece of your everyday job. Strategy is a necessary component, but gamesmanship and inauthenticity are not. In the next chapter, we'll look at specific strategies to build and leverage relationships. I think you'll be pleasantly surprised at how naturally these strategies can be woven into your work life.

For now, I'm asking you to reflect upon, and perhaps broaden, your perspective on networking and building relationships. In the course of my interviews, strong leaders described their perspectives in interesting ways. For example, consider Jennifer McCormick's perspective.

> Think of networking as a productive, useful, necessary part of your professional career rather than just going out to have drinks with people. Networking is just about how you show up, wherever you happen to be. Are you really curious about learning from the people around you? Networking can also be defined as being friendly and challenging yourself to meet three new people in any setting. It's not speed-dating for professionals, so don't worry about showing up perfectly.

7. NAVIGATE THE AMBIGUITY
    THAT COMES WITH CAREER GROWTH

While rapid change is a permanent reality in every job, the role of an individual contributor is relatively stable and clear cut— at least compared with other roles. With every step up the organizational ladder, things get more complicated and ambiguous. At the highest levels of an organization, leaders must navigate their way through a maze of different, and often conflicting, points of view and priorities. They need to influence others, gain support for their plans, and compete for scarce resources.

As they grow their careers, leaders need more and more knowledge, insight, and vantage points about things inside their organizations, within their industry, and across the globe. Given career and industry niches, there's no way to study enough to gather the needed information, let alone the support needed, to get big things done. The best leaders rely on strong networks to meet all these needs. Research shows that when it comes to meeting these needs, the size of the network isn't as important as its composition. The most effective networks are diverse, including people very different from the person at the center.

I hope I've convinced you that a strong network is essential to anyone who wants to grow her career. If you are wondering how to get started building a network that's just right for you, keep reading. As we make our way through the chapters in this book, I'm confident that you'll discover that building a great network is more manageable than you might think. In the next chapter, you'll discover specific action steps to get you on your way.

CHAPTER 3

HOW SMALL CONVERSATIONS CAN LEAD TO BIG RESULTS

Mentoring is a mindset more than a relationship with a specific person. Mentors are all around you. They are the people who engage in conversations that help you think about things differently, who are available to answer your questions, can act as a sounding board, give advice, or provide ideas and insights that are different from your own.

Don't think about mentors as people in authority but people you can reach out to and learn from. Mentors are any people who can help you in areas in which you need to develop.

— Amy Gonzales

These words from Amy Gonzales, Vice President of Global Learning and Development at WUI, do a nice job of articulating our perspective on mentoring and networking.

From this perspective, as I've already mentioned, most of your mentoring relationships will be not be formal, although some may be. A mentoring relationship may be a long-term relationship that evolves and morphs over time, or it may involve a single conversation. As Susan Sobbott says, "Sometimes the best mentor is just a voice or piece of advice you need to hear."

I love what Tony Hunter, past CEO of Tribune Publishing and a long-time mentor and sponsor for WUI, says, "Don't just rely on one mentor. Be greedy. Get many."

At WUI, we encourage our participants to embrace this broad perspective on relationships. Above all, we encourage intentionality. A successful leader doesn't sit around waiting for a manager or human resource professional to craft her career. While she may enlist both for support, she takes responsibility for her own career and for building her own network. Her relationship needs change over the course of her career, but the need for a network never ends.

As you'll discover in this chapter, that network may involve a board of directors, sponsors, peers, subject matter experts, junior associates, and more.

When it comes to expertise in the area of relationships at work, Kathy Kram, a professor in management at Boston University, deserves special recognition—and our attention. At her first job after graduate school in 1975, Kram had her first mentor, one of the few women in a senior management role at the time. This leader took Kram under her wing and was the first to point out to her the importance of knowing yourself, your passions, and your talents, and using that knowledge to make "considered choices" in the steps of your career. This mentor coached Kram on how to navigate what was a considerably uneven playing field for a woman at the time.

When Kram decided to pursue a career as an organizational consultant, she began a doctoral program. A few pages on the importance of a young man having a mentor in Dan Levinson's *Seasons of a Man's Life* caught Kram's attention. This launched her on her dissertation and a program of research and inquiry that has lasted throughout her career. That career includes her 35 years as a faculty member at Boston University and authorship of multiple books on developmental relationships.

Along the way, Kram's perspectives on mentoring have naturally evolved—in part because of advances in the field and in part because of her own maturation and experiences. Kram considers herself fortunate to have had connections with people who have been instrumental in her growth, advancement, and well-being at every stage of her career.

In her early career, Kram researched cross-gender mentoring as well as mentoring in general. More recently, she has studied peer mentoring and then what we at WUI call a personal board of directors. In Kram's world of academia, these are called developmental networks. Her 2018 book, *Peer Coaching at Work: Principles and Practices,* co-authored with Polly Parker, Douglas (Tim) Hall, and Irene Wasserman, delves deeply into this topic.

A personal board or developmental network is a subset of your broader group of connections, consisting of roughly five people to whom you turn for support and advice in your everyday life at work. These are people that you have *enlisted*—who have a sincere interest in your development and who are qualified to assist you in a critical aspect of your learning and development. These individuals may or may not know each other; they may work in other departments, organizations, locations, or industries.

In speaking of her research in this area, Kram notes an important finding: "The best developmental relationships, whether peer-to-peer or hierarchical, are reciprocal and mutual in terms of who is learning and growing." These are high-quality relationships that are characterized by trust and mutual learning.

According to an article titled, "How Leaders Create and Use Networks," by Herminia Ibarra and Mark Lee Hunter, success in building an effective network begins with understanding that there are three distinct but independent types of networks: operational, personal, and strategic.

An operational network is straightforward; it's the one you need to do your job. This network may include direct reports, superiors, and peers within an operational unit as well as internal influencers who may have power to support or derail a project. It may also include suppliers, distributors, customers, and other stakeholders.

Ibarra and Hunter point out that all managers need this kind of network just to get the tasks at hand completed. To rely exclusively on operational networks only, however, is a mistake. Most of these networks occur within an organization, and the connections are based largely on routine and short-term demands. Also, such networks fall short of asking strategic questions, such as "What should we be doing?" When a manager moves or hopes to move to a leadership role, that individual must reorient his or her network "externally and toward the future."

It's necessary for aspiring leaders to engage in personal networking, which involves seeking out people with shared interests outside their organizations who can help them indirectly with their operational tasks. Such people can be found in professional associations, alumni groups, and other special interest groups. The value of the relationships comes with referrals, information, coaching, and mentoring. In joining a professional association, individuals signal that they are eager to stay current, learn, and support one another in accomplishing professional goals. This allows for an ease of approachability not found in other settings.

While personal networking expands an individual's reach, especially with knowledge and connections, Ibarra and Hunter remind us that leadership success requires more. Leaders must know how to leverage connections in organizational strategy. Leaders need connections with people holding different perspectives, backgrounds, and goals. They must operate with finesse in the face of influencers and coalitions, persuading others to endorse their ideas and competing for scarce resources.

The authors explain the critical shift from manager to leader, from functional to strategic, like this:

> What differentiates a leader from a manager, research tells us, is the ability to figure out where to go and then to enlist the people and groups necessary to get there. Recruiting stakeholders, lining up allies and sympathizers, diagnosing the political landscape, and brokering conversations among unconnected parties are all part of a leader's job. As they step up to the leadership transition, some managers accept their growing dependence on others and seek to transform it into mutual influence. Others dismiss such work as "political" and, as a result, undermine their ability to advance their goals.

For those ready to build a network or reorient or expand the network they currently have, Kathy Kram and co-author Monica Higgins do an excellent job of outlining the broad-brush steps in an article called, "A New Mindset on Mentoring: Creating Developmental Networks at Work":

1. Know yourself first
2. Know your career context
3. Enlist potential developers
4. Regularly reassess and adjust

STEP 1:
KNOW YOURSELF FIRST

Research shows that the makeup of a person's developmental network determines the value of that network. Yet, many people don't know whom to reach out to—because they don't fully know themselves.

Kram and Higgins encourage you to know your personal goals, strengths and weaknesses, preferences, talents, and personal vision for the future before you reach out to others for help.

> Only with this self-awareness will you be able to figure out who to turn to for developmental support in order to further your own personal and professional journey . . . and only then, will you be able to appropriately respond to and engage in the developer's suggestions effectively.

In addition to your talents and skills, you need to assess your relational skills, including,

> Your propensity to reach out for help, your ability to identify potential developers, your capacity to initiate conversations with individuals who do not know you, and your openness to share your own experiences, inviting feedback, and to establishing a connection of mutual trust and respect with another. If you need to strengthen any of your relational skills and/or your self-confidence, consider what you can do to develop this foundation of self-knowledge and emotional competence as you begin forming your developmental network.

STEP 2:
KNOW YOUR CAREER CONTEXT

Once you know what type of job or career fits your talents and passions, it's time to examine the context of your current and aspirational career. If you are seeking to advance in your current career path within your company, you'll need to know how promotions happen in your organization as well as who the formal and informal influencers are. You'll want to explore which of these influencers or sponsors might be open to building a developmental relationship with you.

Avoid the temptation to shortchange this work or you may waste energy or go down the wrong path. For example, one of the women I interviewed for this book described a situation in which she had begun to build a relationship with a potential sponsor. She then discovered that the potential sponsor had a poor reputation within the organization. It became important to distance herself from that relationship.

If you want to change firms, sectors, or industries, you'll need to seek out connections that can provide the information and referrals you need. It will be especially important to understand the established process for moving forward in the target firm, sector, or industry.

Retired President and CEO at Calisolar, Sandy Beach Lin, talked with me about her first management job as a regional sales manager for American Cyanamid. Lin, who did not have a technical background, had to learn all of the technical aspects of her product lines on the job. She knew that if she could represent the company well technically, she could go far. During the earliest part of her career, Lin worked to establish relationships with technical resources inside the company. Tapping into the knowledge these individuals had was essential for succeeding at her job.

At the same time, Lin had decided that she wanted to move within American Cyanamid, which would be a challenge. She says,

> This was a company where moving around between businesses was uncommon, so when I started to move beyond that very early stage of technical growth in my career, I realized I needed to build wide relationships inside the company. And then I needed to learn how to build teams.
>
> If I wanted to move from the chemicals division to medical devices, I first had to literally "make tracks" in that regional sales manager role. They needed to be sure that I could be a good leader of others before they would move me over to medical devices. At that point, I really worked on those lateral relationships, so that when the time came, I could go back and say, "I have performed and made tracks; now I have earned the move over to medical devices."
>
> When the time came, I ended up having three division presidents backing me and agreeing on the move. This was partly because of the relationships I had developed with my peers and others higher in the organization who advocated for me. We didn't call it sponsorship back then, but that's exactly what it was. Relationship building was key to my getting the next job.

STEP 3:
ENLIST POTENTIAL DEVELOPERS

The third step in Kram's and Higgins's process is to enlist the people who can help you get where you want to go. Assuming you want to advance within your organization, these people will include individuals at senior levels who can serve as role models, advisors, and sponsors.

Vice President of Operations at Morton Salt, Jennifer McCormick, from whom we heard in the last chapter, recalls a mentor in her early career at Levi's and then another at Morton's. Each was her manager at one point. These managers were impressed with McCormick's work, and she created a strong bond with each of them. In both cases, when she moved to a different role in the same company, she stayed in contact, and the managers stayed close to her. She says,

> At points when I felt I was starting to stagnate, I would go to them and say, "Hey, I need a bigger challenge; here's what I'm looking for." I used them as sounding boards. Without explicitly having to ask, in both of their cases, they went, on my behalf, to people they could influence in the organization to make sure those people knew about me. My sponsors were able to speak for me through their experience and what they know about me.

But to focus solely on more senior people is short sighted. Your peers inside and outside of your own unit can provide functional information and help you appreciate the big picture, plus give you insight into the politics of the organization and the biases of senior leaders. They can help you test your assumptions and avoid mistakes.

It's also important to develop relationships outside your organization. Amy Nauiokas, in the article "How to Diversify Your Professional Network" cites a study from the 1980s in which Carnegie Mellon researcher Robert Kelly and management consultant Janet Caplan analyzed the characteristics of exceptional engineers at Bell Labs.

Kelly and Caplan discovered that a difference in IQ was *not* the distinguishing factor between top performers and average ones. The distinguishing factor involved how the engineers approached their jobs. Nauiokas wants to make sure we understand the surprising distinguishing factor among this group of elite scientists and engineers: "The most productive employees proactively develop[ed] relationships with other experts—and these networks were significantly more diverse than their average-performing colleagues."

Nauiokas continues,

> More recent research supports the notion that people who are connected across heterogeneous groups and who have more diverse contexts come up with more creative ideas and original solutions. Author Frans Johansson explores the idea of "intersectional thinking" in his book *The Medici Effect,* proposing that the best ideas emerge from the collision of different industry insights.

As you work to diversify your network, think about building connections with those who help you learn, formally and informally. Connect with professional organizations and industry forums inside and outside of your area of expertise. And connect with those younger and less senior than you.

For example, Sheila Jordan, CIO at Symantec, meets regularly with a group of executive women in technology in Silicon Valley. She also deliberately forges contacts with college students serving as summer interns, knowing that young people entering the workforce have fresh ideas and ways of working. Jordan needs access to that information to keep growing as a leader. Like other senior leaders, Jordan tries to keep her finger on the pulse of emerging trends. The best leaders want to be leading the curve, not following it.

Step 4:
Regularly Reassess Your Developmental Network

Kram and Higgins remind us that as an individual's career evolves, the ideal network for that individual will evolve as well. Relationships in existing networks shift and new connections are needed.

As I mentioned earlier, Richard Boyatzis, who was Annie McKee's mentor while she was in graduate school, became her peer. When I asked Kathy Kram about a mentor who had a profound impact on her development, she told a similar story.

Kram met Tim Hall (official name, Douglas T. Hall) when she was a new faculty member at Boston University. Hall was recruited as a tenured faculty member that same year.

Kram describes the evolution of their 30-year relationship:

> At first, Tim was definitely a mentor who helped me understand the ropes of university life and careers. He was a big advocate of my work, so he sponsored me by telling people about my work. He gave me a lot of feedback, positive feedback primarily, to help me develop self-confidence that I had what it took to do the work and to be regarded as an expert in the field.

> So he had a profound effect on my identity as a scholar and an educator, and then, probably about 10 years into our relationship, when I was tenured as well, we were at a meeting together and Tim introduced me as his peer mentor. It was a very significant event because he was basically saying to me, "I'm learning as much from you as you're learning from me and we are now peers." It gave me permission to feel that I occupied a more authoritative, senior role in the academy, and it gave me strength

to express my views and to put myself out there for various opportunities.

That has continued over time, and as we have each faced different decisions along the way, we have consulted each other, so Tim is very much like a peer mentor now. I just finished a book with him and two other people called *Peer Coaching at Work*. We explore the nature of reciprocal learning relationships with people who are comparable, not necessarily in terms of age, but in experience, time in a career, or current phase of life. There's something that causes two people to find a connection in which they can really learn from each other if they have the right attitude, self-understanding, and social skills to do so. That's what our recent book is about.

As I bring this chapter to a close, I find myself going back to the opening quote from Amy Gonzales:

Mentoring is a mindset more than a relationship with a specific person. Mentors are all around you. They are the people who help you think about things differently, who are available to answer your questions, who can be a sounding board, give advice, or provide ideas and insights that are different from your own.

Don't think about mentors as people in authority but people you can reach out to and learn from. Mentors are *any* people who can help you in areas in which you need to develop.

If you adopt this mindset and work your way through Kram's and Higgins' steps, you will be well on your way to establishing the developmental relationships you need to grow your career. Remember to follow Tony Hunter's advice:

"When it comes to making connections and developing mutually supportive relationships, don't limit yourself to a few—be greedy." At the same time, be strategic. For a well-rounded web of relationships, think in terms of your operational, personal, and strategic needs.

If you are looking for specific strategies to make those connections, keep reading. In Chapter 4, you'll learn to evaluate your readiness, set goals, initiate conversations, and broaden your exposure.

CHAPTER 4

EVEN BUSY PEOPLE CAN BUILD POWERFUL NETWORKS

We should always have three friends in our lives—one
who walks ahead who we look up to and we follow; one
who walks beside us, who is with us every step of our
journeys; and then, one who we reach back for and we
bring along after we've cleared the way.
— Michelle Obama

Assuming that I've made a compelling case that networks and feedback are essential to a successful career, you are probably looking for specific steps to build your network. You want to know exactly *how* to approach a potential mentor or request feedback from an executive, peer, or technical expert in another department. Consider the following eight steps:

STEP 1:
MAP YOUR CURRENT NETWORK

Assess the state of your current network by creating a network diagram or map. Here's how:

> Using a white board or blank sheet of paper, place your-
> self in a circle at the center and illustrate how your rela-

tionships radiate from that center circle. Consider the various segments of your life, including family, work, neighborhood, college or fraternity, professional associations, religious affiliations, community services, clubs, and more. Think back and include past connections.

This map is a starting point for you. Identify those individuals in your network who are scorekeepers and/ or influencers. Notice the people who might be able to share interesting perspectives, aid in specific areas of development, or help you move to your next position. Notice which relationships you've allowed to lie fallow and wish to reinvigorate. Notice the individuals whom you might be able to help.

STEP 2:
EVALUATE YOUR READINESS TO LEVERAGE RELATIONSHIPS

Chances are you'll discover some gaps in your network and recognize the need to reach out and grow your relationships. Before you move forward, take time to evaluate your baseline readiness, including your performance, attitude, and receptivity.

STEP 3:
CHECK YOUR PERFORMANCE

No matter the size or scope of your network, the foundation for success is achieving star-level performance status, as defined by the influencers or scorekeepers in your organization and industry. Figure out who those people are and the key areas they value. What are *their* standards for star-level performance? Evaluate your own performance against these standards and adjust accordingly. As Jean Otte used to say, "How do you get the boys to pass you the ball? Show them you know how to play the game."

STEP 4
CHECK YOUR ATTITUDE AND MOTIVATION

In their article "Learn to Love Networking," Tiziana Casciaro, Francesca Gino, and Maryam Kouchaki explain that most people have a dominant motivational focus. Psychologists point out the difference between approaching any given task, including networking, with either a "promotion" or a "prevention" motivational focus.

If you have a promotion focus you approach networking with thoughts about the growth, advancement, and accomplishments that networking can bring you. If you have a prevention focus, you view networking as a professional obligation rather than an activity that will help you meet your goals.

The strong leaders I interviewed for this book all demonstrated a promotion motivational focus or mindset. As you evaluate, and perhaps adjust, your own mindset, consider the following statements from my interviewees:

Jack Yurish

The most important contributor to my progress was my attitude of continuous learning. Another was my attitude of continuous improvement. Both helped me to stand out and be perceived as a leader.

Susan Sobbott

Whenever I met someone new, I was very inquisitive and focused on talking about the business issues I was dealing with. I was always looking for resources, connections, and relationships to understand how the business could perform better.

Courtney Collins, a senior director for a Cisco company

> One of the biggest things is to get over the DIY (do it yourself) mentality. Being resourceful has always been valued in my family. So, there is this DIY mentality that I think a lot of women share. Learning about the value of relationships has actually helped me rewire my brain in many ways.

STEP 5:
CHECK YOUR RECEPTIVITY

For most people, seeking out feedback, at least initially, is intimidating at best. At worst, it feels like a set-up for humiliation. Sheila Heen and Douglas Stone, co-authors of *Thanks for the Feedback: The Science and Art of Receiving Feedback Well*, help us understand why. Our strong and resistant feelings emerge because feedback strikes at the "tension between two core human needs—the need to learn and grow, and the need to be accepted just the way you are." Because of this, even well-meaning suggestions can trigger feelings of anger, anxiety, and even profound threat.

In times past, Heen and Stone, also co-authors of the well-known book, *Difficult Conversations*, focused on training leaders to give feedback effectively. Eventually, they realized that great skills in *giving* feedback are useless in a relationship in which the other person is unable to *receive* or absorb that feedback.

They suggest you consider your typical emotional reactions to feedback. Are you inclined to instantly defend yourself, strike back, get teary—or step back and consider the validity of the feedback? You can't get rid of your automatic reactions, but you can manage them.

Regardless of the strong feelings that may arise, try to think of any feedback you receive as information. It's just data. You always have the right to evaluate its validity and respond appropriately.

Step 6:
Set Specific Strategic Goals

Jennifer Williams, Strategic Project Manager for the Voice of Customer Individual Solutions Group at Prudential, began her career at the company at a young age, managing a team that included individuals twice her age. While somewhat intimidated, Williams knew it was best to be straightforward about the situation and acknowledge that she had neither the knowledge nor the experience to succeed on her own. She sought input from her team about their passions and priorities for their jobs. After weeks of observing and listening to her team members, Williams looked for guidance from her managers. She says, "I got used to looking for guidance early and often right off the bat, and not being afraid to ask for that."

After a number of years, Williams shifted from managing a team to occupying a strategy role in which she has full responsibility for projects within a matrix reporting relationship. Her current goals for developmental relationships are intentional and specific. Williams seeks to have two or three relationships in her immediate organization at Prudential. These are people who see her work on a consistent basis. They observe her interacting and presenting her views both formally and informally. From these individuals, Williams requests feedback that will help her tactically.

Williams also seeks relationships within the company with one or two people who are outside of her immediate organization. With these individuals, she talks more openly about her career goals and progression. She chooses people who understand Prudential's culture and can give her unbiased insight, guidance, and feedback. Because they aren't involved in her day-to-day activities, these individuals can challenge Williams to think about things from different perspectives.

Williams told me a story about an informal relationship she has with a woman who has progressed at Prudential for 20-plus years, gathering much experience and insight along the way. Because this woman was open and honest with Williams in their early encounters, the younger woman has reached out to the senior one with career questions over the years. Williams says,

> There have been times when she has been the one en-couraging me. She's also been the canary in the coal mine, so to speak, saying, "I hear what you are saying, but let's really think about this. Why don't you take X, Y, and Z into consideration first, and then let's talk in a cou-ple of weeks?"

As a third set of relationships, Williams seeks to maintain some significant connections with people completely outside of her industry. She recommends being picky and restrictive in choosing these relationships, saying,

> I want individuals who "wow" me and exemplify things that I am actively working on or who demonstrate skills that aren't yet my strengths. I am eager to observe, initi-ate discussions, and learn from these folks. It's important to me that these individuals have a strong executive presence and take intelligent risks. I want to build rela-tionships with people who are willing and able to articu-late and give thoughtful feedback.

Finally, Williams embraces an emerging role in mentoring others. Some of these relationships occur naturally, and others come via recommendations. Williams appreciates how much she receives as well as gives when she is the mentor.

Courtney Collins agrees that mentoring others should be part of a leader's game plan. She talks about the cyclical nature of relationships and remembers a tip she learned in our LEAD program:

> You always need three types of mentoring relationships at the same time. You need one or more mentors above you who can advise you regarding where you want to go. Peer mentors can help you as things are happening in the present, and you need to be mentoring someone to share the knowledge and experience you've gained. It's a bit like having three generations at the dinner table. I'm always looking to identify my three generations because the learning is so valuable at every level.

> When I look at my leadership journey as a whole, it can start with, "I'm a rock star," and it really ends with the quote from Lao Tzu, "When the best leader's job is done, the people say, 'we did it ourselves.'"

Williams and Collins may define and articulate their networking goals a bit differently, but there is no denying that each of them is intentional. As I've conducted research and interviewed strong leaders, I've been impressed by this same quality of intentionality again and again.

Even if you are intentional by nature, at the early stages of your career, thinking about building your network can be intimidating. Reaching out, especially to more senior people, can leave you feeling one-down and needy. Start by formulating goals based on the type of relationships that will best help you grow and prepare for your next career step. Then, take the first step in implementing your plan. As with any effort, with each step forward, the next gets easier. Your career is worth it.

STEP 7:
ASK QUESTIONS AND INITIATE CONVERSATIONS

Here is a piece of good news: All you need to get started building your developmental network is a good question or work-based conversation.

None of the leaders I interviewed recommended approaching someone with a request for them to mentor you or join your developmental network. Instead, they recommended approaching someone with a question or a perspective and asking for feedback. For example, when Jennifer McCormick was presented with a new challenge, she would go to her manager and say, "Here's the problem. Here's what I think I need to do. Can you give me feedback on how that sounds?"

Presenting a point of view allowed McCormick to demonstrate her competence while asking for feedback and support. It allowed her manager to see McCormick's learning process and contribute to her growth. This became a productive pattern in their conversations.

Susan Sobbott suggests a similar strategy. She tells people to bring a business problem to a conversation because "most people are eager to noodle a business problem." As the conversation or relationship moves on, you can broaden the scope to include more personal career-related issues. Beginning with a business problem or challenge is a comfortable way to start conversations in multiple situations. At a networking event, for example, you can ask, "How does your department or company approach this challenge? You are likely to get a better discussion going with this question than with one about the weather."

Courtney Collins leveraged one conversation at work into an important developmental relationship. As part of WUI program, Collins set up an interview with an executive who was familiar with her work. The executive took the request for an interview seriously and used the time to provide some coaching.

The executive had noticed that Collins had developed a presentation style that was misaligned with the person she was, meaning that she was showing up in an inauthentic way with clients. Other people either hadn't noticed or hadn't the courage to give Collins this feedback. She recognized that if the executive could see that she was presenting in a contrived rather than natural style, others could see it too. Collins received the executive's feedback as a gift, as it allowed her to shift to a style more authentic to her.

The relationship might have ended with the interview and that one piece of valuable feedback, but Collins took the initiative to maintain contact. She thought about ways to remain visible, including moving to the executive's physical building and working from there. She made sure to have consistent touchpoints with him over time, via email, a ping, or a message. She believes the consistency has made the difference, even if the interactions have been short. This individual has become an executive sponsor to Collins. It all started with a simple interview—and remained because of careful follow-up. Sometimes a senior person will notice your work or potential and reach out to build a relationship—but it doesn't make sense to wait around for that to happen. It's your job to manage your career, and typically, you'll have to take the initiative to maintain the relationship.

As you build your network, look for opportunities to have short interviews with executives, peers, people from other departments, and industry experts. Most people are surprisingly willing to share information. And you may not have to make the request on your own. For example, Jennifer Williams went to her mentor with a question: "I've been thinking of setting up a call with so-and-so. What are your thoughts?" The mentor volunteered to make things easier by making introductions and extending her endorsement.

Recently, shifts at Prudential required Williams to begin working across two different arms of the organization, individual life insurance and annuities. She wasn't familiar with the annuity business or the players involved.

In response, Williams got a list of the key stakeholders in the annuity business and set up 30-minute, one-on-one calls, sometimes inviting her boss to sit in on the exchange. The point of each call was to interview stakeholders about their business insights, their challenges, customer priorities, etc.

With this effort, Williams quickly learned who the leaders in annuities were and what was important to them. And these leaders learned her name and what she was doing in the new organization. Williams said, "Being savvy like that in a nonobvious way is a good fit for me."

As you reach out for connections with others, come to conversations with a question or topic to generate conversation. Also think about what you have to give as well as what you have to gain in the relationship. Even in your season as an individual contributor or young manager, you have plenty to give.

Leaders who are at the mature end of their career continuum report that the most effective and lasting mentoring relationships involve mutual learning, even when the relationships are of unequal status. Strong leaders, as I've mentioned earlier, are characterized by curiosity and a love of learning.

People who are closer to the beginning their career continuum have fresh technical knowledge and are current on changes in work practice. If they demonstrate shared values, ask good questions, and present challenging business scenarios, they help more senior people to stay engaged and current. And everyone, no matter how accomplished, blooms with appreciation and recognition.

Step 8:
Look to Broaden Your Exposure

The one-on-one conversations I've been describing are essential, but they are not the only path to building meaningful relationships. A number of the leaders I interviewed deliberately sought out jobs that exposed them to different aspects of the business and the people involved. Consider taking a strategic assignment for a year or two to broaden your knowledge as well as your relationships. The more you know, the more people in your organization will want you on their short-term and long-term teams. Stretch assignments have multiple benefits.

Another path to relationship building is raising your hand for projects outside your immediate job. People who volunteer to serve on interdepartmental task forces and special project teams, give conference presentations, serve on association committees, and/or give time to charitable causes learn a great deal while forging meaningful relationships. Tiziana Casciaro, Francesca Gino, and Maryam Kouchaki, in an article called "Learn to Love Networking," point out that many studies in social psychology demonstrate that "people establish the most collaborative and longest lasting connections when they work together on tasks that require one another's contributions." They cite research demonstrating that "task interdependence" generates positive energy in relationships. Just choose carefully. Raise your hand for project teams that provide business outcomes, rather than tie up your time in dead-end tasks like party planning or administrative tasks.

Many women decide that, given their responsibilities to family, they can't broaden their exposure outside of work with social activities. This is shortsighted and puts them at a distinct disadvantage.

Women who do want to participate in after-work activities complain about feeling excluded from their male colleagues' social events—but strong women leaders don't give up. And they don't necessarily take up golf or another activity they don't like.

Knowing that one of the best ways to build relationships is to spend time with people who share common interests, some women form social groups of their own. I read an account of a woman who enjoyed theater. She bought season tickets and invited others to join her. You can ask others to join you in culinary adventures, start a business- or other-themed book club, create virtual special interest meetings, and more. You might ask others to join you in support of a charity or a mentoring program for at-risk youth. The possibilities are endless when you decide to take charge of your own social activities. These activities aren't going to net you a promotion in a few months, but they are likely to pay off in referrals, insights, and helpful career advice over the long haul.

Reaching out in the ways I'm describing may seem forced and uncomfortable at first. Growing often does involve some discomfort. One of the ways that you might evaluate your relationship-building efforts is the level at which you feel some discomfort because you are trying new things and interacting with people who aren't exactly like you.

Chances are that your beginning relationship map will be filled with people who are similar to you. Our natural tendency is to build relationships with people who are like us, those who share our beliefs, perspectives, and skill sets. But research shows that the most productive networks are made up of highly diverse individuals.

According to Amy Nauiokas, founder and president of Anthemis Group, people who are connected across heterogeneous groups and have diverse contacts generate more creative ideas and original solutions than those in homogeneous groups. Nauiokas points to Frans Johansson's idea of "intersectional thinking." Johansson claims that the best ideas emerge from a collision of different industry insights.

Nauiokas says,

> At Anthemis, we've introduced "collabotrarian" groups—people from different roles, business units and backgrounds (gender, race, ethnicity, age, thinking style) who come together to solve tough problems. The purpose of these groups is not to come to consensus. Instead, they serve as a space for healthy debate and divergent thinking, finding ways to reframe a problem and come up with multiple solutions, the best of which may not be obvious.

As you can see, there are plenty of steps you can take to build your own developmental network. Thankfully, you don't have to take all the steps at once. Begin by evaluating your readiness to leverage relationships and then make a plan you can implement one step at a time. Set specific, measurable goals. Practice asking questions and initiating conversations. Look for ways to broaden your exposure and seek relationships with people and groups who see the world differently than you. Take a deep breath and follow Eleanor Roosevelt's advice: "Do one thing every day that scares you."

TEN TIPS TO EXPAND YOUR NETWORK

1. APPROACH WITH A QUESTION OR ISSUE

    It's awkward, and then some, to approach a potential mentor, advisor, or peer with a request to join your network. Instead, approach individuals with a question or issue and ask their input. Come with an opinion of your own and ask for feedback and improvements. Here are some samples:

    *   Can you give me feedback on the presentation I just gave? What can I do to make it better next time?
    *   I have a challenging situation with my team on XYZ project. Here's how I'm thinking I should handle it. Are you willing to give me your perspective on it?
    *   I'd like to learn more about how your unit operates so that I can better understand how my unit's out-comes affect yours. Would you be willing to give me 30 minutes or so to help me understand your priorities?

    The answers to these questions provide information and help you to test the willingness of the person to engage with you. With those who respond willingly and helpfully, look for mutual interests and opportunities to support one another.

2. ASK YOUR MANAGER OR A PEER FOR HELP

    Informational interviews with senior people in your own and other departments are a path to both infor-mation and visibility. You can ask your manager to help you set up a few interviews or ask your peer to help you set up an interview with his or her boss. Carefully plan these interviews to learn the challenges and priorities of these individuals. The quality of your questions will influence how that person perceives you.

3. TAKE RESPONSIBILITY

    Think of it as your job to manage any relationships you
    have with senior individuals. Stay in touch and keep
    them in the loop. Do not expect senior leaders to take
    the initiative or prepare for meetings. Showcase your
    skills by being prepared with a of couple questions or
    issues.

4. TAKE A STRETCH ASSIGNMENT

    Changing responsibilities exposes you to broader
    knowledge and more people. Sometimes a two-year job
    that's not in your expected career path can yield
    knowledge and relationships that change the game for
    you.

5. RAISE YOUR HAND

    Joining a task force or project that crosses depart-
    mental or even organizational lines can yield powerful
    results. The deepest relationships form when you need
    to work with others to achieve a goal.

6. JOIN A PROFESSIONAL ASSOCIATION

    These organizations help you to stay current on trends
    in your profession or industry while allowing you to
    meet a variety of people. Be active. Raise your hand for
    projects. You can build your visibility on a local, state, or
    national level, depending on the network that best
    serves your goals.

7. SHOW UP FOR
    SOCIAL AND PROFESSIONAL OPPORTUNITIES

    Don't allow yourself the excuse of needing to get home
    to take care of your family. Consider every event you
    attend as an investment in your career—you don't
    know when you will meet that one invaluable contact.

8. JOIN OR CREATE A
    SOCIAL GROUP BASED ON YOUR OWN INTERESTS

    You might invite people to join a book club, explore dif-
    ferent types of restaurants, mentor youth, train for an
    athletic challenge, support a charity, or any number of
    things. Look for common interests and build relation-
    ships around them.

9. GET UNCOMFORTABLE FOR THE SAKE OF DIVERSITY

    Explore ways that you can get to know people who are
    different from you. Research shows that we tend to
    seek out relationships with people who are similar to
    us. Research also shows that these are the least effec-
    tive relationships when it comes to stretching our crea-
    tivity and gaining new insights.

10. REMIND YOURSELF THAT YOU HAVE A LOT TO GIVE

    Consider yourself a wealth of resources, even if you are
    at the beginning of your career. Senior people enjoy
    helping individuals who raise challenges and face those
    challenges with intelligence and vigor. They also need
    younger people in their networks to help them stay cur-
    rent. And everyone is bolstered by appreciation and
    recognition.

CHAPTER 5

THE FINE ART OF BEING VULNERABLE AND RECEPTIVE

> *Getting useful feedback can be the fastest route to growth and improved performance. It's not always an accurate reflection of who you are—it often isn't. But it is always an accurate reflection of how you're perceived. And knowing how you're perceived is critically important if you want to increase your influence as a leader.*
>
> — Peter Bregman

> *Feedback is your relationship to the world. If you get good at receiving feedback, it doesn't just change you. It changes how other people see and experience you.*
>
> — Sheila Heen

In an article called *"How to Ask for Feedback that Will Actually Help You,"* Peter Bregman tells of an incident in which a colleague asked for feedback and then immediately shut the conversation down. Bregman had just co-facilitated an extended training session for senior executives of a large financial services company. Bregman was an outside consultant; his colleague and co-facilitator, whom he calls Mary, worked at the company.

After the training session, Peter asked Mary if she had feedback or could give him advice on how he might do better in this situation the next time. Mary shared some insightful and practical tips and then asked Bregman if he had feedback for her. It happened that Bregman had three suggestions that might be helpful to Mary.

As soon as Bregman began talking, however, Mary interrupted and began explaining all the reasons she had acted the way she did. Mary clearly didn't want the feedback she had just asked for. Given that Mary was more of a client than a colleague, Bregman did not push back. The conversation ended right there.

We don't have enough information to estimate the cost to Mary of missing Bregman's feedback. Maybe it was a big deal, and maybe it wasn't.

I have more than an inkling, however, of what it would have cost Jean Otte if she had behaved like Mary and shut the conversation down in her first opportunity for feedback from Jack Yurish—and Jean almost did.

Shortly after the group of five new executives took over leadership of National Car Rental Systems in 1987, Jean made a presentation to them. Yurish, who was one of the executives, noticed that Jean's style didn't match that of the conservative executives. Jean's style included a lighthearted approach that involved stories and fun. Yurish said,

> I could see as she was making her presentation that our guys were looking at her with frowns, as if to say, "Who is this dippy blonde?" I could see that she was not cutting it with these guys, and yet I knew that Jean was a valuable resource for the company.
>
> I followed Jean out after the meeting and asked if I could talk with her. She said, "What?"

> I said, "May I give you some feedback?"
>
> She answered, "No."
>
> I started to turn away, and then Jean said, "What?"
>
> I talked with Jean about the fact that she had a lot to offer as I viewed it, but the way she was presenting herself, at least to these guys, was not going to be effective with them. That's how our relationship really started. Later, Jean admitted that at various times in her life, her most dreaded question was, "Can I give you some feedback?"

This conversation that almost didn't happen and the relationship between Jean and Yurish that followed was certainly a turning point in Jean's career. Yurish became Jean's long-term mentor and sponsor. He supported Jean as she grew her career and as she launched WOMEN Unlimited. Yurish remains a good friend and contributor to WUI today.

When I think of the ripple effect of this one conversation on the many women Jean mentored between 1987 and her death in 2018—as well as on those women who have come through our programs—I'm overwhelmed. I'm so grateful that Jean chose to listen to Yurish's feedback, particularly when I reflect upon my own career and where I would be without the ripple from that conversation. But we have to remember that listening to and receiving that feedback wasn't easy for Jean, at least at first.

In a similar vein, I would have paid a high price if I had been unwilling to receive the feedback I got from Don, the engineer who was the first to tell me how I was perceived—and, like Jean, I almost rejected the opportunity to hear what he had to say. When I stopped to listen as Don told me that everyone in management thought he could do the human relations job I was performing at the plant, it hurt. Yet, I quickly understood that Don was right. Afterwards, I completely shifted the way I communicated my value. I believe a great deal of my success is a result of that shift.

If feedback is so valuable that it can make or break your career, why is it so scary? Why do we ask for it and then run away from it?

As I mentioned earlier, Douglas Stone and Sheila Heen, co-authors of *Thanks for the Feedback*, tell us that feedback is, by nature, a clash of two core human needs. Feedback has the power to help us learn and grow, and we know learning and growing enriches our lives and our job satisfaction. But even constructive advice suggesting that we might do something better indicates that we aren't perfect. This information conflicts with our need to be accepted and respected as we are. From my own experience and the stories of leaders I've interviewed, I know that maturity helps us be more receptive to feedback, but it's always painful to learn of our faults.

Amy Gonzales had a personal and painful journey opening herself to feedback. She had a lifelong practice of hiding any trace of vulnerability. Chances are that habit was appropriately protective for her as a child, but she came to realize this practice was limiting her personal growth as well as the contributions she could make. She says,

> For most of my life, I had a notion that I needed to be guarded; I needed to get things right; I was unwilling to show any vulnerability because vulnerability was dangerous. Part of it began to change when I had children and realized that keeping myself shut down wasn't going to work for my kids. I also realized that I was in the habit of intellectualizing everything. I could run rings around others at intellectualizing, but I had nothing happening at the gut level.

Knowing that I needed to change, I went on a personal retreat. I asked myself some hard questions, such as, What else should I be doing? What more can I do? In response, I had a visceral realization of "It's not about doing more. What I need to do is let go. I have to let go. And what am I willing to let go of?"

I experienced something akin to a vision of having to put down my shield and suit of armor that had protected me for my whole life. The armor was heavy, and it was not serving me anymore.

Once I could take off that armor, everything changed. My relationships changed; my career changed. Everything changed.

The theme of learning to let go of the need to show up as a "finished product" emerged in a number of my discussions with female leaders. For example, Gonzales said,

I had to let go of the notion that I needed to show up perfectly. I had to accept that there is strength in vulnerability. As a person who was a fiercely independent individual contributor, I came to understand that needing to have all the answers and have everything figured out was limiting in every aspect of my life. The recognition that it was in my own best interest to be more open, more willing to share not just what my strengths are, but also where I need help, was a huge shift.

This reminds me of the work of Brené Brown, the researcher who so eloquently shines a light on the value of vulnerability about our imperfection and willingness to ask for help. She says, "Daring greatly means the courage to be vulnerable. It means to show up and be seen. To ask for what you need. To talk about how you're feeling. To have the hard conversations." Gonzales told me a story of a hard conversation, a time when the feedback she received was hard to accept. It occurred early in her career at a high-tech company. Gonzales, who always prided herself on being a team player, was given feedback that she wasn't operating as a team player after all. Her first reaction was to feel hurt, angry, and confused. Then she stepped back and asked a lot of questions. She says,

> When you have feedback that doesn't align with what you believe or what you think of yourself, it's natural to have an immediate reaction. Then you have to take a step back and process it; you have to get curious. Being curious allowed me to go back and ask questions of my manager, who was a very strong leader. I said, "Help me understand this." And I started to recognize that the problem was that fiercely independent piece of me.

> While I was a team player in that I was always willing to help others, I wasn't reaching out for help on projects because I didn't want to bother people. I thought I had this. I didn't need their help. So, while I was always good at being on someone else's team, they didn't see me as being as inclusive. I wasn't keeping people in the loop. I wasn't as transparent with my thought process as I needed to be. That was a big *aha*. I've had many similar experiences with feedback.

This story reminds me once again of Brené Brown's work. Brown's words succinctly describe a challenge most women, perhaps most people, face:

> One of the greatest barriers to connection is the cultural importance we place on 'going it alone.' Somehow, we've come to equate success with not needing anyone.

Many of us are willing to extend a helping hand, but we're very reluctant to reach out for help when we need it ourselves. It's as if we've divided the world into 'those who offer help' and 'those who need help.' The truth is that we are both.

I love that Gonzales used her curiosity to try to understand feedback because, as you know, curiosity is a key attribute of a strong leader. Research shows that women get less feedback than men, and that the feedback they receive is frequently vague and ambiguous. Whether we like or dislike the feedback we receive, whether we understand it or not, if we want to grow, we must learn to be curious. Unlike Mary in the opening story in this chapter, we need to say, "Tell me more. Help me understand. Give me an example."

Jack Yurish suggests three questions to dig deeper into feedback: 1) What do you mean? (ask for specificity); 2) How do you know? (ask for validation); and 3) What difference does it make? (ask for relevance).

I think of curiosity as a muscle we can develop with exercise. When people disagree with me, especially if things get intense, I practice going to that person and saying, "I just want to understand how you see this differently." I take the same approach when I get feedback that I don't immediately agree with.

Expressing curiosity and asking probing questions not only helps us get better information—which we can then accept or reject—but it also changes how others view us. They see us as people who value their opinion and who want to grow.

When I asked Ann Groccia to tell me how she responds to feedback she doesn't immediately agree with, she answered, "I work on trying not to be defensive—to sit with it and try to understand it." As an example, she shared an incident from our own relationship at WUI.

Groccia came to me feeling she had too much to do and couldn't complete everything on her plate. She remembers my saying something to the effect of, "Okay, but you took all these tasks on yourself. You said yes." Groccia remembers being disappointed at my response. She says,

> I had to sit with that information and realize that you were right. I had put myself into this overloaded situation. It is my responsibility to think through and prioritize what I'm doing, decide what's important, and what's not important. I should not always be saying. "Oh, yeah, I'll do that," and "Oh, yeah, I'll do that too."
>
> If you see yourself as a doer, it's a hard thing to identify which things are not for you to do and step back from the request. That's been a really good learning for me, especially in a small organization like WOMEN Unlimited. It's so easy to take on too much and allow good ideas to crowd out the important. So that was good feedback for me, but I had to really reflect on it before I could accept it.

Of course, not all feedback is on target; it's just data that we need to evaluate. Courtney Collins told me about a time she was working on a difficult project in which things weren't going well. As things unfolded, she decided to go into a virtual meeting that she hadn't been invited to—with her guns blazing. She felt proud about standing up for herself and believed she was doing it in a respectful way.

An executive on the call, however, saw things differently. He waited until the end of the meeting and provided some feedback. He said that Collins was being neither collaborative nor a team player because of the way she had shown up in that meeting. Then the executive abruptly got off the call. Collins says,

> I got this feedback and I was just so upset. I was in tears, and I reached out to my paid executive coach to help me think through options about what could be going on. And when I calmed down and expanded my horizons, what I realized was that the executive didn't like what I said, and he didn't like the way I said it. And that's okay! But it was really difficult because of the way he gave the feedback.
>
> We talk about feedback as a gift, feedback as just data. You can choose whether or not you believe the source; you can choose whether or not you want to take the data in or not. I still got so affected by this, and it was a great lesson. I asked questions and leveraged other relationships in order to make sense of it. When I did make sense of it, I realized that the executive's reaction might not have even been about me, and I got to choose how I responded to it. This put me in a more empowered place to think about that feedback.
>
> Since then, I have engaged and enrolled this executive in my daily work and we've never had to address the incident because I don't feel the need to anymore. Now we actually have a good working relationship, and it's interesting to me that in choosing to come from an empowered place and to seek the lesson of the feedback, I've been able to learn from it, and I can still leverage that relationship too.

When you are taken by surprise or you get feedback that feels like a punch in the gut, try to respond politely, knowing that you don't have to process the feedback right then and there. Jenny Williams says,

> When I get feedback that surprises me or is especially critical, I say, "Oh, I didn't even realize I was doing that or coming across that way." If I happen to be by myself or reading the feedback via email, I let myself take a moment to react naturally.
>
> Maybe that means my feelings are hurt initially. Maybe that means I question the feedback and I'm skeptical about it. I might wonder who the person giving the feedback thinks he or she is to give that feedback. I might think, "That's absolutely not true." I get my hurt and anger out of my system if I can, if I'm in an environment where I can do that.
>
> That clears my head, and once I let those emotions go, I'm able to pause and think critically about where the feedback is coming from. Can I think back to an example? Do I need more information? Do I need to find out if anybody was impacted by this? Do I need to take action?

When Sandy Beach Lin gets feedback that surprises her, she tries to remain neutral, even as she acknowledges her surprise. She advises: "Listen, take a deep breath, and, as much as possible, thank the person for the feedback."

Lin believes that how a person reacts to feedback is highly individual. For her, it's important that she remembers who she is, what she has accomplished, and that growth requires all pieces of herself—her strengths, her weaknesses, and the true areas for development. She says, "And so, I've taken feedback and utilized it for my own growth. Over the years, I've also reached out to my supporters when I need encouragement or the occasional kick in the pants."

Because all human behavior, including feedback, takes place in a cultural context, it's wise to seek out organizations and workgroups that are open, transparent, and positive. Individuals who work in organizations that foster a culture of frequent and honest feedback seem to have less intense reactions to negative feedback than those who don't. I think these individuals learn to process feedback as a route to improve specific behaviors rather than as a global criticism of their person. They learn how to separate their self-image from an indication that they need to improve in a specific area or behavior.

I reached this point myself (at least for the most part) through some early conditioning. As a young girl, I took dance lessons, like many other young girls. After several years, I transferred to a more professional dance studio where I took tap lessons. During my classes, which were semi-private, I got plenty of attention from the instructor. In fact, I consistently heard all the things I was doing incorrectly.

I have memories of the instructor tapping his cane, indicating I was to snap my tap. If I was off beat, he would tell me what I was doing wrong. When my posture was poor or my turns were not crisp, I heard that too. All these comments were to help me "see" what I needed to do to improve—to meet my goal of becoming a professional dancer.

While I never became a professional dancer, these lessons served me well when I entered the business world. I recall my first board meeting, in which I was to present my recommendations for the company's benefit plan. This was my first management role and my first encounter with our board. I had worked very hard to develop an effective strategy.

Shortly after I began my presentation, the board members started asking me questions. It was clear to me that they were not pleased with my recommendations. I realized I had made an error. I had failed to find out what their expectations were! I immediately started asking them questions to gain a better understanding of their perspective, and I asked if I could return the following month with a revised proposal. The board members agreed.

Later that afternoon, the company president came into my office. He was concerned that I would be upset about what had happened in the meeting. He was surprised when I said that I felt the board was correct in stating their objections; I had made an error in judgment. They hadn't been disrespectful, they hadn't yelled or cursed, they had merely pointed out their disagreement. Now that I had a sense of direction from the board, I knew I would be successful in the next meeting.

With both my dance instructor and the board of directors, I was able to receive the feedback and strive to improve. After all, both had valid points. Both were providing me with information to achieve my goals. They were giving me the direction I needed to succeed. Of course, it made a difference that, in both cases, the feedback was given factually and respectfully.

Jennifer McCormick has a lifetime of receiving feedback respectfully. In fact, although Jennifer is 50 years old, she considers her father, who is a psychologist, a member of her board of directors. McCormick "taps" into her father personally and professionally frequently. She says, "He is always someone who is very honest with me. He is also the person who taught me the value of feedback."

McCormick's mother and stepmother are also psychologists. She was raised by psychologists! She says,

> I've never been grounded. I've never been sworn at. But we've talked a lot. I've been coached my whole life. The gift of feedback is something I grew up with. I say that as a joke, but it's also very much true. Given the way I was raised, feedback has never felt or sounded foreign to me;

it's never felt scary or off-putting in any way. It's all in
how the feedback is delivered.

Annie McKee agrees that the way in which feedback is
given plays a big part in how easy or difficult that feedback is
to receive. McKee was able to receive feedback from a woman
who had hired her to clean house and iron her clothes because
that woman delivered the feedback in a supportive and respectful way. She says, "When you are vulnerable, it's really important to know that the support being offered is coming from a
human-to-human place, and dignity is absolutely key in that
exchange. It's really key."

Of course, not everyone who offers you feedback is a
skilled communicator. Sometimes even well-intentioned feedback comes through harshly. But unless I have a reason to
think otherwise, I assume a person offering feedback has positive intent. After all, it's generally much easier to avoid giving
feedback than to give it. When I receive feedback, I test the
validity, but I do so with the intent to learn from the feedback if
I can.

Obviously, if someone delivers feedback inappropriately,
by raising his or her voice or making demeaning comments
about you, walk away from the situation, letting the person
know you will listen when he or she can speak calmly and respectfully. You have the right to set boundaries.

But here's the important thing: I can receive feedback as a
gift and still treat it as data. Feedback is information about
someone's perspective. I can get curious and ask questions so
that I can better understand that perspective. I can seek out
other perspectives and weigh one against the other. Once I've
honestly investigated the feedback, I can accept it or reject it. I
always have the right to make my own decision—and so do
you.

TEN TIPS TO RECEIVING FEEDBACK NON-DEFENSIVELY

1. LET GO OF YOUR FIERCE INDEPENDENCE

   Many of us learned to be fiercely independent in our families. After all, it's the American way. The DIY mentality may work for independent contributors, but it is the kiss of death for leaders. The higher you go in an organization, the more you need the contributions of your peers, your subordinates, and those above you. Allowing yourself to need others sets you free to succeed.

2. LET GO OF PERFECTIONISM

   Consider perfectionism the twin devil to fierce independence. Both limit your ability to grow as a leader—and to receive the feedback that's vital to growth. Letting go of these tendencies is both painful and essential. If you hang on to independence and perfectionism, you will receive all feedback defensively.

3. CONSIDER ALL FEEDBACK DATA

   In and of itself, feedback is neutral. It may be valid or invalid, relevant or irrelevant. Test feedback against reality and seek out other opinions. Know that you always have the right to accept or reject feedback.

4. ALLOW YOURSELF TO BE HUMAN

   Feedback will often catch you by surprise, and sometimes it hurts in profound ways. Pretending that you don't have an emotional reaction won't make that reaction go away. Seek to identify your emotion and what's behind it. That will free you up to manage it.

5.   FOSTER THE HABIT OF CURIOSITY

Consider any situation in which someone has a different perspective an opportunity to expand your horizons. Rather than shut things down, say, "Help me understand how you see this differently." If this requires a conversation after a meeting or event, ask for that conversation. Learn to value rather than fear it.

6.   DIG DEEPER

Avoid accepting feedback at face value. Use probing questions, beginning with "Tell me more," "Help me understand," or "Can you give me an example?" Try out Jack Yurish's questions: "What do you mean? How do you know? What difference does it make?"

7.   STEP BACK AND EVALUATE

In the heat of the moment, it's hard to be objective. Give yourself time to step back and evaluate feedback.

8.   ASSUME POSITIVE INTENT

Generally speaking, people who give you feedback are seeking to help you grow. After all, it's usually easier to keep your mouth shut than offer feedback that might offend. Unless you have a reason not to, assume positive intent. If the person speaks to you in a way that is disrespectful or demeaning, refuse the conversation until the person can speak to you calmly and respectfully.

9.   SEPARATE PERFORMANCE FROM SELF-IMAGE

It's easy to allow a comment such as, "You can improve your presentation," to hit you with the magnitude of, "You are a lousy professional." Don't allow yourself to go there. Request specifics and evaluate feedback in light of your strengths and positive contributions.

10. SAY THANK YOU

Feedback is essential to your growth. If you receive it graciously, you are likely to get more of it. What's more, a gracious and thoughtful response leads people to see you as a well-balanced and polished professional. That's good for your brand as well as your growth.

CHAPTER 6

IF RELATIONSHIPS AND VISIBILITY ARE SO IMPORTANT, WHY DO WOMEN HIDE?

> *At the end of the day there are five kinds of capital: financial capital, reputational capital, educational capital, physical capital, and relational capital. I argue that besides physical capital, your capacity to walk, see, and have good health to do what you need to do, relational capital is the most important.*
>
> — Nido Qubein

If Tony Hunter were to tell you the story of his career journey, he might just pinch himself because Hunter still sometimes thinks the whole story is a dream, not something that really happened. His 20-plus-year career with *Chicago Tribune* and Tribune Publishing, now known as tronc (lowercase intentional), began with an entry-level position auditing newspapers. It ended with his becoming CEO of his hometown newspaper—a big one at that. When Hunter left the company in 2016, Justin Dearborn, CEO of tronc, said:

> Over the course of his career, Tony has helped steer the company through a period of transformation and innova-

tion, and we are grateful for the decades we have benefitted from his leadership and expertise.

Tony led the Chicago Tribune Media Group through bankruptcy and a rapidly changing business landscape to become a leading media and marketing solutions company today. Tony has also been instrumental in helping tronc identify innovative strategic partnerships and initiatives to transform the business and achieve our collective financial objectives.

Our company is well-positioned today thanks to the countless contributions he has made.

These are lofty accomplishments for a guy who started at *Chicago Tribune* by driving around in a car, auditing newspapers in the smallest cities of the United States, cities with names like Podunk, Iowa, and Syracuse, New York.

It didn't take long for Hunter to realize that the company's auditing process and the way auditors were treated were not current, relevant, or competitive. Rather than mumbling complaints while doing his job in obscurity, Hunter started speaking up. Management noticed and promoted Hunter. His first managerial task: fix the auditing process.

As I interviewed Hunter in preparation for this book, I was as struck by his humility as I was by his accomplishments. Hunter wanted the record to show that he attributes much of his own success to always having a mentor. He fondly remembers his regular Friday lunches at Wendy's with his first mentor, where the bill for both came to $7.50.

Hunter also wanted the record to show that his 10 years as a mentor with WUI increased his awareness in multiple ways. He grew from the experience as much as he gave. Once his position as CEO made it unfeasible to participate as a mentor in the program, Hunter served as executive sponsor, ensuring that women from the company were always participating in WUI programs and bringing back best practices. The practice became part of the organization's culture.

Hunter is fully aware that women have unique challenges in the workplace. He can only tell his own story and share strategies from his years of mentoring and leading both men and women. I believe his perspectives and advice are worthy of careful consideration.

First, Hunter was quick to volunteer for tough jobs and tough assignments. When everyone else was looking down at their shoes, Hunter habitually raised his hand and said, "I'll do that." In many cases, Hunter hadn't a clue of what he was going to do or how he was going to solve the problem involved, but he volunteered anyway—and then he made sure to deliver.

Second, Hunter intentionally crossed department silos. He volunteered for many cross-department initiatives and took every opportunity to meet people in other departments. He worked hard to show he was a good team player.

Last, Hunter was intentionally outspoken, although he was careful to pick when and about what. Hunter had passion and conviction around his ideas. And when the results were good, he let other people talk about his results.

Hunter was patient, and he was gratified when his boss or his boss's boss would say, "Thanks to Tony for leading. Thanks for that idea." He liked to work behind the scenes and then have others talk about what he had done.

Hunter's business results and career growth were dependent on being genuinely collaborative and knowing how to navigate his own organization. In his view, exactly how to navigate depends on the organization, and that's something every emerging leader needs to figure out.

If you want to grow your career, Hunter advises you to find the answers to the following questions: Who are the power brokers? Who are the influencers? What are the politics? What are the hot buttons that set people off? Once you know the answers to these questions, you can make choices about going against the norms. If you choose to, you can go against the norms purposefully, with your eyes wide open. It becomes a high-risk, high-reward situation.

This is the approach that Tony Hunter—a man—used to gain visibility and grow his career. But would it work for a woman? Would a woman engaging in these behaviors seem too outspoken, too aggressive, and/or too ambitious?

An article published in *Harvard Business Review* in August of 2018, entitled "Why Women Stay Out of the Spotlight at Work," seems to answer "Yes."

In cooperation with a woman's professional development organization at a large US nonprofit, researchers Priya Fielding-Singh, Devon Magliozzi, and Swethaa Ballakrishnen conducted 86 in-depth interviews with women, observed 36 discussion groups, and sat in on 15 program-wide meetings.

The research revealed three primary reasons women choose invisibility at work:

1.   AVOID BACKLASH IN THE WORKPLACE

While the women recognized that being less visible in the office could hurt their chances of being promoted, they were more concerned that "violating feminine norms" could leave them even worse off. For example, a woman who had worked in a male-dominated field for 35 years believed women who take strong or stern positions in the workplace are still perceived as bitches. She didn't want to be perceived that way.

2.   ALIGN PERSONAL AND PROFESSIONAL AUTHENTICITY

Many of the women in the study rejected a self-promoting style as masculine and inauthentic for them. They considered the pursuit of visibility to be self-serving and detrimental to the team. The researchers say these women viewed staying behind the scenes as more consistent with their personalities than taking up space and taking credit. In this way, being less visible helped many women align their personal values and professional demeanor. While this allowed them to carry out their work with authenticity, it also kept their contributions from being recognized.

3.   RELIEVE PARENTHOOD PRESSURES

In this study, mothers proved more likely than other women to choose intentional invisibility at work. Invisibility gave these women more time and energy to complete tasks at home. It also allowed them to avoid the conflict with partners that might come with increased responsibilities and a bigger time commitment at work. Generally speaking, many mothers choose to structure their careers for flexibility to care for children, while their male partners pursue ambitious, and often more inflexible, careers.

The article concludes with a call to organizations to undertake initiatives to make it less risky for women to be visible at work.

Our organizations certainly need to change to allow women to move more easily and productively into leadership positions. I'm not arguing against that. In this book, however, *I'm primarily interested in factors women themselves can control.* When women step up and take responsibility for their own careers, both the women and the organizations in which they work benefit, even as other changes are slow to take root.

Women who first enter our programs at WUI express concerns similar to those reported in the study conducted by Fielding-Singh and her colleagues. But these women are not content to be invisible. They want to advance in their careers, and their organizations are sponsoring them for the same purpose. Some of the work we do with women involves unpacking the assumptions they bring to the program.

We find that one reason women frequently don't speak up about their accomplishments goes deeper than the effort to avoid backlash, although that is often a concern. Many women believe that the value they bring to their organizations is self-evident. They expect managers and others in the organization to be attentive, and, in the light of their excellent work, to arrange promotions. In my early job in human resources in a manufacturing plant, I believed that the value I brought was clearly visible—until Don explained that it was not.

Given this assumption, women often keep their heads down and work hard to meet exacting standards, often thinking it is easier and faster to get the work done independently than to rely on others. For women holding this perspective, being an independent person is an asset, and they might say, "Things would fall apart if I weren't here to hold things together."

This mindset flies in the face of what I've discovered in my research. In fact, the most prominent feature of the profile of a strong leader is the clear understanding that he or she cannot succeed alone. As you know from the last chapter, some of the successful women we interviewed admitted that they hadn't always understood this. They recall reaching a point in their careers when they realized that being fiercely independent was a liability rather than an asset.

Strong leaders are aware of the cultural bias against women who are loud and forceful, but that doesn't mean they don't stand up for their work and their ideas. In his coaching for both women and men, Tony Hunter reminds people that effectively supporting ideas is about timing and patience, not being loud or winning arguments in the moment. Some people think they need to win an argument when a difference first comes up, as if there will never be another discussion on the topic or they will have compromised themselves by failing to speak up immediately. Hunter says,

> I always try to tell people it's about timing; it's about how you present the message and who you present the message to. You need to understand that getting your voice heard isn't necessarily in the moment—and the loudest person or the last one to speak doesn't win.
>
> Success comes from strategically working behind the scenes, finding a champion for your point of view, and then working behind the scenes outside the meeting to get people to follow you and support your idea. With that kind of prework, execution is only 10% of the job. It's not particularly helpful to jump right out at the moment because you feel like your ideas haven't been heard and you've been dismissed.

Amy Gonzales, whose impressive experience developing talent in a variety of industries preceded her work at WUI, says, "Women need to learn how to speak for their work, even with the risks involved." As a team leader and then director in a high-tech organization, Gonzales was responsible for teams below her on the organizational chart. She wondered how she could let her teams, as well as herself, shine.

Gonzales believed that shining a spotlight on the team's accomplishments would create a reflection on her own. So, she reported on how the team members put strategy in place, how they made headway, and how they achieved results. In her view, achieving visibility involves understanding your own role and then fostering accomplishments in a way that is neither at the expense of others—nor at your own expense. You talk about accomplishments in a way that promotes your own brand and accomplishments, but also promotes whatever team members have been part of the effort. This is a strategy that can work for anyone who believes in collaborative relationships in the workplace.

In speaking of yourself or your team, Gonzales believes it is essential to shine your spotlight on the most important information: results. Here is how she puts it:

> Women tend to spend more time talking about activities than they do results and impact. We need to understand what organizations care about, and how successful people talk about those things at work.

> The language of business is a language of impact, numbers, and quantifiable results. Women need to get better at saying something other than, "I worked really hard, and my hard work should speak for itself." We need to start thinking about what we do in the context of what matters most. Out of all we do, what is it that makes the biggest difference?

Many of those I interviewed emphasized this same point. Both women and men talked about learning the language of business and explaining their work in that language. Strong leaders use the language of business when talking about their career goals and next steps. When they make a pitch of any kind, including the next assignment or job they want, strong leaders explain how that initiative or assignment will enable them to contribute better to the company.

In order to do this, they need to know how the organization keeps score, and what it measures. Jack Yurish says, "Just as in any sporting event, a contributor needs to understand what constitutes a score. Successful people always start there."

The curiosity we find in so many successful leaders is an asset here. Those who cross department lines, build diverse relationships, and seek to know how different aspects of the business fit together have a better understanding of the scorecard than others.

There's no better way to understand the scorecard, however, than ensuring that you have job experience with P&L responsibility. This is essential for your visibility and credibility as well as your realistic working knowledge. Women who sit on the sidelines don't get noticed or promoted, and arguably, they don't deserve to.

*****

When we start talking about scorecards at WUI, many women just entering our programs say that they want to be a contributor but are insistent about not wanting to "play the game." As the research of Fielding-Singh and her colleagues found, the idea of playing, manipulating, and strategizing for visibility feels like compromising authenticity to many women. Rather than feel personally inauthentic, many women opt for intentional invisibility. This is an incredible loss of talent for organizations and an incredible loss of fulfillment and satisfaction for brilliant and competent women.

At WUI, visibility, risk, and authenticity are frequent topics for discussion. In fact, these topics are so important that I've devoted a chapter to each of them, although, as you might expect, the discussions naturally overlap. The focus of this chapter is visibility, but authenticity is naturally part of it.

Chapter 7 focuses largely on taking strategic risks for your career. Chapter 8 is about authenticity, particularly as you move into the murky waters of leadership roles.

Regarding visibility, Jean Otte was known to say, "It's not what you know, it's who knows what you know." She wasn't talking about knowing the movers and shakers so that we could ask them for favors. She meant that we need to keep certain people in the loop so they know we are contributors in terms of how the organization keeps score. Being realistic about the score is not selling out. It may require some flexibility, but it doesn't require changing who you are.

Best-selling author and Senior Fellow at the University of Pennsylvania, Annie McKee, PhD, has been a rare female leader in her field. She describes herself as being "counter-normative in the corporate world in the '80s, '90s, 2000s." She says,

> There was a uniform, which I knew very well how to put on. And I knew which outfits would allow me to still be me. I know how I need to show up to be accepted by tenured chaired faculty who've been here forever. And I know exactly who they need me to be. And I know which parts of that I can do without losing my soul.

Of course, women entering corporations today have a different set of requirements surrounding uniforms than women did when McKee began her career. When I asked Courtney Collins about what she has done to establish visibility and a brand in her organization, she told me a story about pink hair!

Collins, who currently works at a new, agile startup, always wanted to have bright pink hair. But she was afraid to act on this desire in a corporate setting. Then, with what she calls some bravery and authenticity, Collins dyed a couple of chunks of hair pink during a holiday break. She did this in a way she could hide the chunks if needed in front of customers. She says,

> Because it was authentic to me and I did it for all the right reasons, my pink hair ended up becoming part of my brand within the company. People weren't offended by it. They actually loved that it helped this kind of legacy tech company. My look made sense in the way management wanted to move towards a new, more innovative startup company.

It felt good to be memorable for her pink hair, but Collins soon realized that she wanted to be known for something more meaningful. She says,

> As I've grown in my leadership journey, I've reached a point where I want to become known for the meaning that I bring to things. I want to be known as somebody you call in when there's a new idea, vague topic, or a creative deliverable. I do quite a few different things right now to try to establish that visibility and that brand.

While many women are choosing intentional invisibility, Collins is strategically and systematically creating the type of visibility and brand she wants. How does she do it? Collins identifies a few key influencers at a time and strategizes about how she can interact with those influencers in ways that make her memorable in all the right ways. She thinks of everything, from how to show something different when she has the opportunity to present, to what she might say if she runs into a key influencer in the breakroom or elevator.

Collins once worked for a CEO who was notorious for asking people on the elevator, "What have you done to add value to our company today?" Collins learned to be intentional about preparing for such interactions and "collisions" that might happen in person, virtually, or even through email. She says, "I do a lot of tactical planning around how I am going to influence these key individuals, and then tick, tick, tick, the box every time."

*****

It's important to address the evidence that Fielding-Singh, Devon Magliozzi, et al., uncovered regarding women choosing less demanding jobs to relieve parenting pressure. It's tempting to blame the gender inequities behind this on the highest levels in the organization. I'm convinced that doing so is a distracting oversimplification. For starters, not all women have children, and many who have children find ways to get tasks at home taken care of.

Robin J. Ely, Pamela Stone, and Colleen Ammerman describe their survey of more than 25,000 Harvard Business School graduates in an article called, "Rethink What You Know about High-Achieving Women." Their results suggest that "the conventional wisdom about women's careers doesn't always square with reality." Here's a telling excerpt:

> The pull of child-rearing has long been a dominant explanation for the small proportion of women in corporate boardrooms, C-suites, partnerships, and other seats of power. For years before Lisa Belkin's 2003 *New York Times Magazine* cover story added the term "opt out" to the cultural lexicon, senior executives were assuming that high-potential women who quit their jobs were leaving to care for their families.
>
> In the early 1990s, Mike Cook, then the CEO of Deloitte & Touche, thought this was why only 10% of partner candidates in his firm were women, even though Deloitte had been hiring equal numbers of men and women for the

preceding 10 years. But when Cook convened a task force to look behind the numbers, he learned that more than 70% of the women who had left the firm were still employed full-time one year later. Fewer than 10% were out of the workforce to care for young children. The vast majority of female employees who left Deloitte did not jettison (or even pause in) their careers; they simply went to jobs elsewhere.

The research showed that some mothers quit their jobs because they were pigeonholed after taking a maternity leave or a spell in part-time work. These women quit their jobs because they became bored. At the same time, the surveys found the following:

> Most women who have achieved top management positions have done so while managing family responsibilities—and, like their male counterparts, while working long hours. Women want more meaningful work, more challenging assignments, and more opportunities for career growth. It is now time, as Anne-Marie Slaughter has pointed out, for companies to lean in, in part by considering how they can institutionalize a level playing field for all employees, regardless of gender or caregiver status.

> Companies need to be vigilant about unspoken but powerful perceptions that constrain women's opportunities. The misguided assumption that high-potential women are "riskier" hires than their male peers because they are apt to discard their careers after parenthood is yet another bias women confront.

Our research at WUI and the interviews I conducted for this book reveal that, despite biases, women *can* take control of their careers and achieve leadership positions, even while balancing family responsibilities. I'm not suggesting it's easy, but I am suggesting that we needn't give up in the face of cultural and institutionalize bias.

Annie McKee made it to the top of her profession as a single mother. Susan Sobbott interviewed and was selected for an executive position when pregnant with her first child. Sandy Beach Lin had her first child while working as an international product manager for medical devices at a conglomerate called American Cyanamid.

Lin had wanted to work part-time, but the company did not want to set a precedent at that time. Lin left and was going to stay home for a while. While she was participating in a playgroup with her daughter, a job in the biomedical industry "found her," enabling her to continue building her career while working part time. Years later, she served as President and CEO of a Silicon Valley start-up before moving on to serve on multiple boards.

If you want to advance in your career, reflect on your attitudes toward independence, visibility, and "playing the game." Sitting back and blaming others for failing to notice your outstanding work won't get you where you want to go. You'll need to learn to talk the language of contribution and develop strategies so that influencers will hear you and reward your results. Those strategies will likely involve some risk. Keep reading to learn how some amazing women have taken risks to advance their careers. You can do it too.

CHAPTER 7

STORIES OF COURAGE AND GROWTH: HOW WOMEN STRATEGICALLY TAKE RISKS

You can't be that kid standing at the top of the waterslide, overthinking it. You have to go down the chute.

— Tina Fey

No one who knew Jean Otte would describe her as passive, mild, or risk-averse. She worked hard, promoted her cause, and achieved many "firsts" as a woman in business. Jean was passionate about paving a smoother road for the women who followed her.

As an example of her sheer nerve, you'll recall the story of how Jean handled one of her first encounters with the group of five men who took over National Car Rental. In preparing to go before the group, Jean's boss said, "Whatever you do, say as little as possible and hope to get out with your job."

If she really was in danger of losing her job, Jean decided to go down fighting. According to Jack Yurish, who witnessed the event, Jean gave a presentation before the group that basically said, "I am head of customer relations, and I am one of the most important people in your company."

The chairman asked, "Why is that?"

Jean replied, "Because, I talk to your customers every day, and I know what this company needs in terms of what they do well and what they don't do well." She added, "As you can see at the top of this chart of my organization, the title says vice president."

The chairman asked, "Well, what are you now?"

Jean answered, "Director. And I might add that I'm the only director who doesn't get a car."

The chairman said, "Duly noted; come up here and sit next to me." Jean sat next to the chairman for the rest of the meeting.

Knowing she was in front of the organization's new influencers and decision makers, Jean took the opportunity to showcase the unique value she brought to the company. In a customer service company, a person who has access to what the customer needs and wants is an important player in the game. Jean had that access, and she made sure those five senior executives knew it.

Jean was gutsy, but she was also human. During her years at National Car Rental, Jean and Yurish often talked about Jean's dream of starting WOMEN Unlimited. She was well aware of the obstacles involved in bringing this dream to reality.

Yurish recalls,

> As we were discussing the concepts of WUI over many nights, Jean would repeatedly say, "Well, but I couldn't do that."
>
> I would say, "Why not?"
>
> Then, as we talked further, she would say, "Oh, I don't think that's possible."

I would say, "Why not?"

The question for me was always, "Why not?" For every objection Jean had, I would say, "Let's talk about it. Why not?"

We kept chipping away at the objections. At one point, Jean said, "I'm never going back to New York."

Of course, New York is exactly where Jean went to start the program.

When objections are holding you back from a dream, a change, or a promotion, it's important to engage in interactions in which you are encouraged to question why you're resisting, why you're objecting. Most of our resistance is in our heads, and we often fester there and miss important opportunities.

When someone asks us, "What good is your festering doing you?" it can spark us to consider the issue differently.

As with visibility, the majority of women who enter WUI programs are initially hesitant about taking risks. Research shows that women typically *are* more risk-averse than men. The behaviors that stem from this hesitancy play a role in holding women back. The hesitancy may manifest itself in hunkering down, overanalyzing, and slowing things down. These behaviors are then perceived as non-leader, because in our culture speed and boldness are admired. Nancy Parsons, author of *Fresh Insights to End the Glass Ceiling,* goes so far as to say that women take themselves out of the running. I'll share more about Parsons's findings later in this chapter.

Like it or not, careers do not grow without risk-taking. Each of the successful leaders I interviewed told me stories about their risks—some easy and small, others scary and large—but they didn't always label their choices as risk. Sometimes the individuals simply saw themselves learning or building essential skills.

For example, immediately after graduating from college, Courtney Collins moved from the United States to London to get some international work experience, taking an internship with the London Stock Exchange for no pay. Collins lived on 25 pounds a week from her savings in order to get this unique experience. That decision has served her well.

After the internship, Collins accepted roles that allowed her to help diverse people bridge the gaps between the knowledge they were lacking and the people they didn't know. Initially, Collins did this by helping US companies find funding in the European markets. Then she worked at an executive briefing center in London for a company that was later acquired by her current company. She's been presenting in the executive briefing center to customers now for the last 10 years, finding that the skill sets she developed in each job have enhanced her performance at the next. Her successful career journey all began with a decision to embark on an adventurous learning experience, a calculated risk.

Collins is not the only one who undertook adventures or job changes in search of building knowledge and skills. Ann Groccia tells me she took a particular job at Fidelity because she was ready for a stretch assignment. She had become tired of what she was doing and wanted to stretch. Of her time at Fidelity, Groccia said,

> I had always been the relationship management person. Salespeople made the sales, and then, once a customer had said yes and signed the contract, that customer became my responsibility. I had a solid grasp of the relationship management piece, but I didn't know how to

sell. I wanted that skill, and so I consciously went looking
for it. I came to WUI because I wanted to develop sales
skills.

Groccia's story illustrates once again that successful leaders are strategic about their careers. Groccia did not wait for a
boss or human resource manager to offer a promotion. She set
a goal of where she wanted to go, determined what was needed
to get there, and took the needed action. Successful leaders
own their own careers.

Owning your career means strategically building your core
skills, expanding your responsibilities, and expanding your
network both inside and outside your organization. For some
people, this happens during a natural career progression in one
organization. For others, it happens through volunteering for
assignments outside their daily job opportunities. For others
still, it requires changing companies.

Aspiring leaders do well to raise their hands. For example,
you'll remember that Tony Hunter's first and foremost strategy
was to volunteer for the tough assignments, not necessarily
knowing as he raised his hand how he would succeed. He just
made sure he did.

Sometimes raising your hand involves leading a project
that crosses departmental boundaries, and at other times it involves accepting or pursuing a lateral move in order to increase
your functional knowledge. I encourage you to think about the
opportunities that arise, but I also add a word of caution.
Women need to raise their hands for *strategic* volunteer opportunities, not dead-end ones. Researchers Linda Babcock, Maria
Recalde, and Lise Vesterlund discovered that women are prone
to volunteer in ways that hurt rather than help their careers. They
explain why in a *Harvard Business Review* article called "Why
Women Volunteer for Tasks that Don't Lead to Promotions."

Tasks that don't lead to promotions are ones that are time-consuming but unlikely to drive revenue or be recognized in a performance evaluation. While these tasks may need to be done, they aren't relevant to the scorecard. As such, these tasks are unlikely to advance a person's career. Examples include serving on low-ranking committees or task forces, filling in for a colleague, organizing a holiday party, or routine work that doesn't require much skill or make much impact. Which tasks constitute non-promotable tasks varies across industries, but they tend to be agreed upon and understood within an industry.

Babcock, Recalde, and Vesterlund designed an experiment, controlling for a number of factors, to learn why women agree to do non-promotable tasks at a higher rate than men. Participants consisted of 696 University of Pittsburgh undergraduates who were divided into groups that received a reward if someone in the group volunteered to click a button on a computer screen. The averaged results of 10 rounds of the experiment with mixed groups revealed that women were 48% more likely to volunteer than men.

The researchers conducted a second experiment with single sex groups to test for differences in attitude toward risk or altruistic motives. It turned out that in single-sex groups, women were no more likely to volunteer than men. The researchers came to the following conclusion:

> These results suggest that the real driver was a shared understanding or expectation that women would volunteer more than men. In a mixed-sex group, men will hold back on volunteering while women in turn will volunteer to ensure the task is done. But in single-sex groups, this changes—men and women volunteer equally. In these groups men know they have to step forward if they want to find a volunteer, and women

expect other women to volunteer, making them less
compelled to do so themselves.

To dig a little further, the researchers designed a third experiment in which a group manager was shown pictures of the
group members and asked to click on the picture of the person
he or she wanted to ask to volunteer. Here are the results:

> Women received 44% more requests to volunteer in
> mixed-sex groups. Intriguingly, the gender of the manag-
> er did not make a difference. Both male and female
> managers were more likely to ask a woman to volunteer
> than a man. This apparently was a wise decision; women
> were also more likely to say yes. A request to volunteer
> was accepted by men 51% of the time and by women
> 76% of the time.

These results bring us right back to the need for strategy.
Successful leaders voluntarily raise their hands for tasks that
1) help them learn and develop new skills; 2) show up on the
scorecard in meaningful ways; and 3) help them build relationships and visibility throughout the organization. As you know,
Jean often said, "It's not what you know; it's who knows what
you know." Successful leaders have the courage to say no to
tasks that will keep them busy and out of sight.

Jennifer McCormick's career journey is an example of
how as a leader she built core skills and increased her visibility
with each job change she made, some of which were lateral
moves. Working for Levi Strauss just out of school, McCormick became a supervisor, got coached by a strong boss, read
lots of books, and developed her people skills on the job. She
became the supervisor of a bigger team before taking on the
role of night shift supervisor. That job led to a facility leadership role as a director of a distribution center with P&L respon-

sibility. Over time, McCormick became director of two distribution centers as well as some logistic providers—about 1,100 people in all. She describes the first 10 to 12 years of her career as leadership on steroids, years during which she learned to build relationships and work with people to meet goals. With each step, the role got bigger and bigger, and so did the risk, the accountability, and the opportunity to influence.

When she could go no higher within the Levi Strauss structure at her Midwestern location, McCormick had the opportunity to move to a leadership position in customer service at corporate headquarters in San Francisco. That change and move weren't easy for her. From there, she took another role in sales and ultimately led the men's and boys' sales teams for Levi's and Dockers.

From that vantage point, McCormick could see how each of her positions was building upon the core skills she had already developed. Now she was leveraging her functional experience and relationships in a new part of the organization as the lead sales chair. As the lead in sales, she was gaining a greater understanding of overall P&L, appreciation for the brand, and a marketing perspective.

Eventually, McCormick turned down a promotion opportunity with Levi's in order to live near family. This was a difficult decision that led to her taking a job at Morton Salt where she is now vice president of operations.

The 30-plus year career journey of Sandy Beach Lin provides another example of how taking assignments that increase your knowledge and contribution to the scorecard creates visibility and opportunity for advancement. Lin's journey involved a number of jumps from one company to another.

As an MBA graduate, Lin accepted a job with a conglomerate in a yearlong program designed to give participants diverse experiences throughout the company. Knowing that a path to full P&L responsibility was in the sales and marketing area in that company, Lin next worked as sales representative, selling rubber chemicals to the tire companies over a five-state area. From there she became a product manager in that company's chemicals division, with responsibility for multiple lines of chemicals. That was an international job, so the world literally opened up to Lin at that point. She was then promoted to regional sales manager for the plastic additive division. In this, her first management role, Lin was responsible for sales in half of the United States.

As you know from a previous chapter, Lin was able to persuade the company to transfer her to the medical device division, something unheard of in that company. This was possible because of the strategic ways in which Lin built both her skills and her relationships. She created the path to where she wanted to go.

Lin thought she would be with that company for many years, but that was not to be. Lin made the risky decision to leave and stay home for a while following the birth of her first child because the company would not allow her to work part-time. Soon after, when she was in a playgroup with her daughter, Lin says, "A job found me."

Lin became the vice president of a biomedical division for a small company that represented multiple products. She worked part-time until after the birth of her second child, then Lin left that company and stayed home for a year.

After that year, the Lin family relocated to the Midwest, where she had deep roots. Lin accepted a marketing role in a company making surgical gloves. Within 10 months, she got an offer to join Allied Signal and move to Singapore. She led the specialty wax business for Allied Signal (which later merged with Honeywell), creating a structure from scratch in Singapore. Lin spent several years in that role. After she successfully performed in Singapore, Lin was promoted to the corporate headquarters where she held a director role responsible for multiple product lines.

Lin became the vice president and general manager of the specialty wax business for Allied Signal. After a couple of years, she was promoted to President, Bendix Commercial Vehicle Systems, a truck brake business in the company's automotive group.

Lin then had the opportunity to go to Alcoa, with responsibility for 28 beverage closure manufacturing plants around the world. A few years later, Avery Dennison recruited Lin to lead a group of businesses. In terms of dollars, the size of Lin's responsibility kept increasing at each step.

After three years at Avery Dennison with five different businesses reporting to her, Lin was asked to move to Dallas to lead the engineered materials business for Celanese Corporation. Her responsibilities grew to include two other businesses, or roughly half the company. Following this role, she moved to California to lead a startup called Calisolar. She now serves on multiple corporate boards.

When I asked Lin to share some of the strategies behind her impressive career growth, she recommended the following:

- Strive for execution and outstanding performance. In other words, be really good at what you do.
- Build great teams, because the word spreads and you attract the best people.
- Show up early. At times, you'll get extra facetime with important people simply because you are in the room together before an event starts. Lin believes an incident like this was a factor in helping her get a big role.

- Close the loop. Be known as a person whom others can count on to get things done and close the loop. Don't leave things or people hanging.
- Ask for what you want. When you want a role or responsibility that opens up, communicate your desire clearly.
- Be curious, demonstrate a genuine interest in others, and listen well.
- Take challenging assignments. Certainly, there is risk in this strategy, but succeeding in challenging assignments helps you be very visible in a positive way.

Obviously, a challenging assignment has the potential to derail a career as well as catapult it. I asked successful leaders for their advice about how to evaluate an opportunity. Lin said,

> It is important to think about the resources and allies that you have inside the company. You should look at any challenging assignment holistically; for example, what happens if it doesn't work out? What are the risks?
>
> As you're looking at the upsides of, "Hey, I'm going to do this and I'm going to do it really well," look at the risk around the downside also, including the fact that you might lose a job. Ask yourself, "If I need to go look for a job, what would be the financial picture for myself and my family?" You really need to think these things through if the opportunity has a high risk to it.
>
> When we picked up the family and moved to Singapore to create this new role in Asia, we hit on all cylinders. It was literally the best thing for my career. I think it catapulted me faster than I would have been able to do on

my own on a more traditional pathway. But I needed to thoroughly weigh the risks before I took that job.

When evaluating any opportunity or any directional decision, be sure to leverage your network both inside and outside the company. The more diverse your network—including people who know you well, people who know your company, and people who know the industry and/or marketplace—the more valuable that network will be when it comes to evaluating a change or challenge.

If you feel hesitant about accepting new challenges, you are in good company. Generally speaking, women demonstrate more hesitation than men about taking risks, and therefore need more encouragement. Several of my interviewees shared stories that shed light on this.

A female mentor who was two grade levels above Jennifer Williams called to ask if she had applied for a specific open position. When Williams responded that she was aware of the open position but hadn't applied, the mentor pushed for the reason.

Williams responded, "I'm not qualified. Look at what they are asking for."

The mentor explained that, statistically speaking, women will not apply for a job until they are confident they meet 80% or more of a job's qualifications. Men, on the other hand, will apply for a job when they have 40-60% of the qualifications. The mentor finished by asking Williams, "Why do you think there are more men in leadership roles than women? They're holding themselves back."

Susan Sobbott tells a similar story. During a significant and growth-oriented career at American Express, Sobbott had the opportunity to become president of what was then called American Express Small Business Services. Although the job was clearly within her abilities, Sobbott intended to turn the opportunity down. She was a new mom still trying to figure out how to get everything done, and she planned to have a second child. Sobbott thought it all might be too much.

That's when a valued member of her network, Jean Otte, stepped in with a challenge. Jean told Sobbott that her male colleagues would not be responding in the same way. Her male colleagues would take the job, figuring that if it didn't work out they would do something else. Realizing this truth, Sobbott took the job and thrived. In fact, Sobbott grew the business dramatically, changing the face of American Express within the small business community. By the time she left that business, it had quadrupled in size and was the fastest growing part of the business.

But the advice a woman needs isn't always a push forward. Sometimes the best decision is to leave an opportunity on the table. For example, Courtney Collins was at one point considering moving into a traditional sales job and didn't feel qualified for it. She reached out to people in her network and did informational interviews, requesting opinions about her fit for that role, and asking for tips or tricks and any other advice they had for her.

Members of her network thought Collins would do a good job in the role, but they also shared relevant information about the job itself. The job required repetitive administrative tasks, very accurate forecasting, and standing up for those forecasts in front of challenging people. When Collins considered all the information, she realized that she was not naturally good at the tasks required of the job. While she could learn the tasks, she wouldn't enjoy them. Collins says,

> By leveraging those relationships, especially with people that knew me and could identify my strengths and skill-sets, I was able to see all the things that I would have ab-

solutely hated about the role. I got to a place where I
knew I didn't want the job.

Sometimes "fit" is about more than being qualified. If
you are open, curious, and trainable, as many people are
today, you can learn to do different skill sets and you can
learn to do them very well. For me, changing jobs has not
been as much about feeling qualified as it's been about
whether I feel ready to move into something else. I can
get past the qualified pretty easily, but the feeling ready
has been probably a bigger mountain for me to climb.

Conducting the interviews in preparation for this book, I
was struck and sometimes overwhelmed by the courage of the
participants. Stepping forward and taking risks seems so natural to them. From Annie McKee getting her doctorate as a single mother to Jennifer McCormick switching from Levi's to
Morton Salt, to Susan Sobbott building a sales group from
scratch in Singapore, as well as all the rest, these are strong
leaders.

Chances are, these powerful women had their moments of
self-doubt and hesitation, as we know our founder Jean Otte
did. The truth is that such moments are especially common to
women. Successful leaders, male and female, learn to overcome hesitation, in part, with the support of their networks. Pay
attention to this admission by Amy Gonzales:

Over the years, I've had to push myself, particularly when
I'm under stress. If I'm in a stressful situation, I tend to go
internal. My natural inclination is to go reflective, go in-
trospective, and sort of huddle down. And that's where
I've had to really push myself through over the years. I've
learned that the time when I want to go dark is the time I

most need to reach out to others. If there's uncertainty, I need to hear from my network.

If I have a career choice or decision to make, I think about who is most likely to say what I don't want to hear, who will say, "Stop. You know how to do this."

Sometimes I need the cheerleaders and the supporters; sometimes I need the people who are going to ask me the tough questions and work things through. Either way, it is knowing who in my network, who among the people that I consider to be mentors for me, that I can ask. The asking part is simple. The asking part is picking up the phone. When I think about mentoring relationships in my network, it's always fostering those relationships. It's always being able to pick up and say, "I have a question. I need to bounce something off of you." I love doing that.

Nancy Parsons, CEO of CDR Assessment Group, and her team uncovered evidence that the female tendency to hunker down under stress is a contributing factor to the glass ceiling effect.

CDR offers a suite of scientifically validated assessment tools that are used for a wide range of leadership development and talent management applications. A breakthrough finding came through analysis of the instrument known as the CDR Risk Assessment. This instrument measures eleven inherent or hardwired personality risk factors or ineffective coping strategies that undermine performance and can derail success. All of us have risk factors or dark sides of our personalities that show up in times of stress.

Results from a CDR study of 35 companies revealed that under adversity and conflict, women are statistically more likely to be "worriers" than men. Scoring high on the worrier scale indicates that a person is unwilling to make decisions for fear of failure or criticism. Worriers impede progress by digging in, working harder, and overanalyzing.

You might remember that Jennifer McCormick describes herself as a "recovering worrier." She spent so much time in the evenings analyzing and worrying about things that she got to the point that she wasn't sleeping well, that is, until she realized that she could bounce her plans off her boss and ask for feedback. This strategy seems to work for her. After all, she is vice president of operations for Morton Salt.

As an example, Parsons shares the story of Diane, a woman I imagine most of us can relate to. Diane returned to school to complete her MBA more than ten years after completing her bachelor's degree.

In an early assignment as an MBA student, Diane was asked to write a paper on a key business issue. Diane spent 40 hours over the next week on this assignment. After work, Diane toiled late into the night and over the weekend to get the assignment done in time. Diane said, "I was worried about what the teacher expected of me, and I didn't want to fail."

Once the papers were turned in, Diane learned that the teacher had just expected her and the other students to spend a couple of hours on this assignment! Diane said,

> As a working person, I had gone into hyper drive because I was worried about getting a good grade on one paper (something that, in reality, would have had a minimal impact on my life or career, even if it had been mediocre).

When behavior like this shows up in the workplace, it obviously slows things down. Others interpret the behavior as indecisiveness, a lack of courage, and failure to adapt to changing demands.

Under conflict and adversity, men exhibit contrasting behavior. In fact, men in the study tended to be "egoists, "rule breakers" and "upstagers," words that need no definition.

Parsons explains how the worrier trait results in women adopting a *moving-away-from-conflict* approach, setting them up to be judged as lacking courage and confidence. Men, on the other hand, tend to adopt a *moving-against-conflict* stance and fight for resources and airtime with aggressive behavior. While women delay the process, men push forward with speed and force. Like it or not, these behaviors are viewed as leader-like by those who decide on promotions. Parsons says,

> Women need to help women stop resorting to their natural self-defeating and self-doubting tendencies and learn ways to manage, neutralize, and prevent the worrier behaviors from derailing their visibility, upward mobility, and success.

She goes on to quote Sheryl Sandberg, Facebook's COO. In *Lean In: Women, Work, and the Will to Lead*, Sandberg says this,

> I also know that in order to continue to grow and challenge myself, I have to believe in my own abilities. I still face situations that I fear are beyond my capabilities. I still have days when I feel like a fraud. And I still sometimes find myself spoken over and discounted while men sitting next to me are not. But now I know how to take a deep breath and keep my hand up. I have learned to sit at the table.

I have a vivid memory of an experience in which I feared I had stepped into a situation that was far—even light-years—beyond my capabilities. It was my husband, a member of my board of directors, who talked me down from walking away from one of the biggest growth experiences of my life.

It happened after the opening event of my doctoral studies in the PennCLO Program at the University of Pennsylvania. This is a three-year cohort program, in which participants learn from each other as well as the materials and professors. Totally intimidated by the caliber and experience levels of my fellow students, I called my husband from my hotel room after the opening reception. I was packing my suitcase as I talked.

I said, "I don't know why you let me do this. The people here are really smart and from all over the globe. The admission folks made a mistake. I don't belong with these people and I think I need to come home." I repeated, "The admission folks made a mistake. I have nothing to offer these people. I need to come home." I was a living example of the imposter syndrome.

My husband listened patiently as I poured out my angst. Knowing me and knowing how important my doctorate would be to the organization, he said, "I hear that you are uncomfortable." Then he asked, "If one of our daughters was saying to you what you are saying to me, what would you tell her?"

Ouch. Knowing what I would say to my daughters and any number of young women, I stayed and worked through my discomfort. I rose to the occasion and now consider the experience one of the most enriching ones of my life—both personally and professionally. I found that I had a lot to give as well as a lot to learn, and the relationships I built continue to bless me.

For example, I met Annie McKee who supervised the program. She provided great support to me as I completed my dissertation. Annie continues to be a great friend and mentor. I met Kathy Kram when I reached out to her while conducting research for my dissertation. I found her to be generous with her time as she shared her expertise on mentoring. As you know, both women said yes when I asked them to share their wisdom with you in this book.

When you have an opportunity to take a risk to further your career, consider the opportunity carefully and reach out to your network for insight. Feel free to turn down an opportunity that is not the right fit, but do not let fear be the factor that holds you back from taking a strategic risk. It's your responsibility to own your career and step forward. Take a deep breath and go for it!

STRATEGIES FOR EVALUATING RISKS

When I asked Tony Hunter to give advice about how to successfully take risks within an organization, he said the following:

> The protégés I had in the WUI program [emerging leaders at *Chicago Tribune*] tended to be risk averse because they overanalyzed or were concerned about making a mistake. If you do all the spade work, all the prep, all the planning—even though it looks like you're jumping off the cliff—I believe there's likely to be a net beneath you. Even if things don't go perfectly, there's probably a net for you. But don't move forward until you've done all the spade work first.
>
> I've found that as long as you're doing your fiduciary responsibility for the organization and getting guidance from your network, board of directors, and mentors, you can take a risk. If you believe that you're acting responsibility for the organization, a new position is an opportunity, not something to cause you to be fearful.

Jack Yurish agrees that fulfilling your fiduciary responsibility to the organization is the key to success. He refers to this as "on-target performance," one of "Three P's" he uses when coaching and mentoring: Performance, People, and Processes.

In Yurish's view, this simple concept constitutes the formula for success in any undertaking, especially in the business environment.

PERFORMANCE

Too often, people focus on activities when they need to focus on results. Enjoying sports analogies as our founder, Jean Otte, did, Yurish says,

> Performance is the end game, the goal. It's a standard of measurement by which everything else is judged. Just as in any sporting event, a contributor needs to understand what constitutes a score. Successful people always start there.

PEOPLE

It is only through people and by people that activities get carried out and results are achieved. Success depends on everyone having the knowledge and skills to play his or her part successfully. A leader needs to ask, "What will it take to successfully play the game and score in a big way?"

PROCESSES

Yurish says,

> All work is a process. Outstanding people with poor processes will not do as well as average people with great processes.

Individuals who aspire to higher levels must fill a toolbox with processes and tools which are helpful and effective when dealing with a variety of challenges.

He recommends identifying processes for critical thinking, problem-solving, decision-making, strategizing, determining priorities, assessing risks, etc. Having effective processes in place is especially important when faced with situations that are ambiguous or have ill-defined boundaries.

Yurish finds Philip Crosby's Process Model especially helpful. This model contains all of the components necessary for successfully analyzing and improving processes. Crosby's books, *Quality is Free: The Art of Making Quality Certain,* and *Quality Without Tears: The Art of Hassle-Free Management,* are classics in dealing with process analysis projects.

Yurish points out that having a toolbox of things that work is a significant source of confidence that will enhance an individual's ability to take risks and step forward into leadership roles and greater visibility.

CHAPTER 8

HOW TO NAVIGATE POLITICS WITH INTEGRITY

Leadership requires different approaches as you go up the ladder. Yes, I'm my authentic self, but sometimes your authentic self can use some help.

— Condoleezza Rice

When I asked Amy Gonzales how she manages to stay authentic as her career grows and changes, she told me about an early experience that delivered a lasting lesson.

Gonzales had just taken a job as a regional training manager when she found herself on a plane headed to a train-the-trainer program. Once there, she was handed a schedule, one that required her to deliver at least two presentations each day, in multiple cities, over a three-week period.

Gonzales will never forget her first session, held near the Seattle airport. She arrived feeling inadequate and uninformed. On a huge stage with a flip chart and a group of people looking at her, Gonzales bombed. She says, "I fell over the flipchart. I literally landed on my ass on the stage. I was so nervous and uncomfortable."

The problem, in part, was that Gonzales was thinking about Sigrid, the person she was replacing, who happened to be a bubbly and polished presenter whom everyone loved. Gonzales kept trying to be Sigrid, and of course, the harder she tried, the worse things got. By the end of the second day, Gonzales was weeping in her hotel room.

Out of necessity, the following day she showed up for her session as Amy Gonzales. Rather than make a fancy stage presentation, she decided to have a conversation with the audience about what the company was trying to do and why it was important. At the end of the session, people came up to Gonzales, saying, "You know, this was really refreshing. For the first time, a message from the stage didn't feel like corporate speak."

That was when Gonzales began to embrace an Oscar Wilde quote: "Be yourself, everybody else is already taken." Gonzales says,

> As you grow your career, you get more confident in who you are; you get clearer on who you are. With that knowledge, you can simply bring more of yourself to the table. It doesn't mean that when you take a bigger position, you change your core self; it's that you come to understand the organization at a different level. Your vantage point changes. What you have to do changes, but it doesn't mean you change who you are.
>
> My values have never changed, and I'm absolutely clear about that. There's no dynamic about the corporate line that feels uncomfortable for me versus who I am, because I represent both.

Because experience tells me that concerns about authenticity can be a sticking point for women who want to advance, I asked each of the people I interviewed to answer the question I presented to Gonzales: How have you managed to remain authentic as your career grows and changes?

While each person answered with a commitment to remaining true to self, each also pointed out the need to be dynamic and flexible. Authenticity and integrity are not static conditions. In fact, most of us need change how we show up as we reach higher levels of leadership. I know I did.

For example, early in my career in human resources, the company I worked for needed to cut costs. The decision to close one of our plants and eliminate several positions at our headquarters had been made. The need to make the recommendations on who should be eliminated was weighing heavily on me.

One day, my boss, Doug, came into my office and asked if I was having fun. I replied "Are you kidding me? You know what I am working on."

"Yes," replied Doug. "You are wearing your worry so that everyone can see it."

Doug's comment and feedback helped me understand the importance for leaders to manage how they show up for others during difficult times. The way the leader shows up sets the tone for how others can move forward. In this case, the need to show up with confidence and positivity was my job as a leader. It didn't negate my authentic compassion for those affected, but it did require that I adapt how I was showing up.

Ann Groccia shared how she realized the need to adapt as her career progressed at Fidelity. Early on, with the group in a startup mode, team members went about their business a bit like a group of cowboys, which was appropriate at that time. As the group became increasingly successful and Groccia moved up the organizational ladder, however, she began to get feedback that her communication style was inappropriate.

Groccia came to learn that her pattern of being argumentative and assertive wasn't working at the higher level. She was being perceived as overly emotional. Groccia says,

> I got a lot of feedback and I had to work on how I was communicating. I came to realize that if I wanted people to listen to me, I needed to take a different approach.
>
> For me, it's always about being heard. If people weren't able to hear me, I had to change how I was presenting myself. That's how I stayed authentic to myself. If I wanted to be heard and be able to progress in my career, I had to change. I figured out how to temper myself.

Jennifer McCormick approaches the dynamics of organizations with honesty, integrity, and clarity about what lines she is not willing to cross. With this as a base, she says,

> Politics is really just another word for the influence you have in the organization, the strategy you use. It is how you communicate, with whom you communicate, and how you present your point of view. It's the words you choose and the actions you take. At the end of the day, politics is about strategy and selling your ideas and your point of view or getting support from other people by using your relationships. As long as you're recognizing what you're trying to accomplish in every conversation, and that's not something deceitful or disrespectful, you are in a good place. I'm not trying to win or have somebody else lose; it's just: "How do I be effective?"

Chances are McCormick would appreciate these words that have been credited to Madeleine Albright: "I have very set and consistent principles, but I am flexible on tactics. I like to get the job done."

Susan Sobbott maintains that failure to be authentic is setting yourself up for big problems. She says, "Eventually you will be miserable, or you will be found out. It's not a sustainable proposition to actually be anything other than yourself. I just always believed that, so I never really tried to do anything differently."

While Sobbott's perspective makes good sense, it doesn't necessarily make things easy, especially in uncertain times. Working for American Express during the recession and credit crisis in 2008, Sobbott was working for a company that was fighting to survive. When she advocated for what she believed was most important for the company, she found herself standing alone. She says,

> I was the person talking about the customer when everybody else was asking: Are we going to be here tomorrow? People were very vocal about how I was missing the point because customers wouldn't matter if we went out of business. From my view, if we stayed in business, we were going to need some customers. It was an interesting moment in time, where I stood alone and felt very alone. Eventually, it all came together and I was appreciated for what I had done. But there were some dicey moments.

In this case, Sobbott boldly advocated directly for what she believed to be the right path. She doesn't, however, insist that this is always the smartest choice. She tells of a time in which she worked for someone who was in the habit of offering untenable ideas in group settings. While Sobbott wouldn't chime in saying, "Gee, that's a dumb idea!" she would ask questions to reveal problems with the idea. Her boss, who was interested in others stroking his ego, didn't like this. Because she was unwilling to stroke the boss's ego, she paid a price in the relationship. Sobbott cautions:

> That's a criticism I would have of myself, that there are times when stroking egos is a good, smart thing to do. It just didn't come naturally to me and it was not something that I was going to do, especially if I felt that it was not going to be helpful for the business.

You'll remember from a previous chapter that Tony Hunter often avoids the clash created by expressing his point of view adamantly in a meeting. He is inclined to bide his time, working behind the scenes to gather support for his proposals. Like Sobbott, however, he is fully aware of the rules in his organization and cognizant of what it costs to break those rules. It's a calculation, and sometimes it is worth the cost to break the rules.

When Hunter answered my question about maintaining his authenticity as he progressed in his career, he said,

> You don't have to have a lobotomy the higher you go in the organization. You don't have to change who you are. You need to build better skills and flex differently. But should you be transparent in who you are? Yes.

> After being introduced as the CEO of *Chicago Tribune*, the first slide I showed was a picture of my family. That's me. I'm not going to tell you how great I am, all the experience I have, and what I'm going to do.

> I think people just need to get comfortable in who they are. Sure, you need to adjust. But deep inside, everyone has great qualities. And why would you change who you are? Just use your best qualities at the right time.

I had my resume ready roughly eight times in my last eight years at Tribune Publishing because I was not going to change being transparent and authentic. If it cost me my senior role, oh well! I knew I was getting results, and people were engaged; they trusted me because I was transparent.

*****

For individuals who pride themselves on getting results, the ambiguity that comes with higher organizational levels can feel both risky and messy. Before Hunter accepted the Publishing Division CEO role, he had a conversation with his mentor about whether he should take the job.

At the time, Hunter was CEO of *Chicago Tribune*, what he considered to be one of the greatest jobs in the publishing industry. He was being asked to add the role of CEO of Tribune Publishing to this job, with corporate responsibilities and several newspapers reporting to him. Happy in his operational role, all Hunter could think about was bureaucracy. He wasn't sure he wanted to step into that.

Hunter reached out to his mentor for advice and vividly remembers the conversation. His mentor literally grabbed Hunter by the shoulders and said, "When have you ever performed a job in the way your predecessor did? You are a change agent!"

This is yet another example of the valuable perspective a mentor can bring to a situation or decision. Hunter had been seeing the ambiguity and predetermined the expectations he would encounter as CEO to be a problem. His mentor helped him see the promotion as an opportunity to shape the corporate CEO role the way he wanted to.

Of course, having an opportunity to shape a position doesn't make it wise to charge in like a bull in a china shop and do so. When situations and roles are ambiguous, and your job requires you to make decisions and take risks, you need your network more than ever. Hunter recommends getting "air cover," meaning that you bounce your ideas off others in the organization who can give you realistic feedback and influence the acceptance of your vision. And, in doing so, you need to present yourself and your ideas in a way that makes clear you are working in the best interest of the organization.

Speaking about the people she relies on as sounding boards to help her in her position as a leader, Sandy Beach Lin says she looks for value congruence—people who espouse her same values, and who have integrity as their bedrock. These elements determine the people she seeks out for developmental and supportive relationships.

It took 20 years and another mentor's insight to help Lin understand how much such a relationship helped her during an ambiguous challenge in her career.

When Lin took on a lead role working for the CEO in Bendix Commercial Vehicle Systems, the group was in the midst of the largest recall in the company's history. The story got a lot of media attention, including a of couple days on the front page of the *Wall Street Journal*, because they were re-calling truck brakes for school buses right when the schools were opening in September. They successfully navigated through the recall with no injuries, and even ended up with a better brand name because of how they handled it.

Relating this story to a mentor two decades later, Lin shared how much she had gotten out of working for that CEO. She explained, "The CEO saw things in me that I didn't see in myself, and he believed in me and my ability, especially as I took on a large P&L role in a division that was in the middle of a big transition.

The mentor observed, "That's because the CEO trusted you."

Lin says,

> I realized that a key ingredient in my success was the relationship that I had built with that CEO over a number of years. He had seen me perform in multiple positions. He was a demanding CEO, but based on our long-term relationship, he trusted me.

Your direct manager is an important individual with whom to build a trusting and honest relationship. In an earlier chapter, I shared the way in which Jennifer McCormick made a habit of presenting her point of view and requesting feedback from her manager at Morton.

When McCormick was unclear about how to move forward in a situation, she would present the situation to her boss and say, "Here's what I think I should do. What do you think?" This created an opportunity for the two to work on something together and for the manager to help McCormick grow and gain confidence in her decisions. It also allowed the manager to see and appreciate the process the emerging leader used to work through problems.

The need to build a trusting relationship with your boss and the associates with whom you work closely is obvious. Achieving the right composition for your entire network is more elusive.

Experts remind us that, left to our own devices, we will limit our networks to those who are both similar to ourselves and readily available. Herminia Ibarra calls these "narcissistic and lazy networks," and points out that networks built on similarity are unable to provide "the breadth and diversity of inputs we need to understand the world around us, to make good decisions and to get people who are different from us on board with our ideas."

In a *Harvard Business Review* article called, "How to Build Your Network," Brian Uzzi and Shannon Dunlap attribute our lazy networks to the self-similarity principle. This is the tendency to develop a network by choosing "people who resemble [us] in terms of experience, training, and worldview, and so on." We build these kinds of networks because it's convenient and because it's easier to trust people who share our perspective of the world. Sharing information with people you see regularly is efficient, and those people are less likely to challenge your ideas. Like-minded people, the authors contend, will typically affirm your point of view and gratify your ego.

A self-similar network becomes increasingly limiting as we move higher in our organization and encounter more complex and ambiguous situations. Simply building a bigger network doesn't solve the problem. People who are most successful in leveraging networks are connected to multiple diverse network clusters. What's more, they serve as the only, or one of the few, links between these clusters.

For example, one person might link a school alumni network cluster with a corporate network cluster, with a professional association cluster, with one comprised of chief technology officers, and another comprised of non-profit community members. Individuals within the disparate clusters have no access to each other without the person who provides the link among them. This person is known as the information broker among the networks.

If everyone in your network knows nearly everyone else, you have an inbred and low-value network. You'll be more successful if you connect to several independent networks in which you are the sole point of connection, the information broker. Uzzi and Dunlap say,

> Too much similarity restricts your access to discrepant information, which is crucial to both creativity and problem-solving. If all your contacts think the way you do, who will question your reasoning or push you to expand your horizon?

Uzzi and Dunlap tell us that "networks deliver three unique advantages: private information, access to diverse skill sets, and power."

1.   PRIVATE INFORMATION

We routinely use public and private information to form opinions and make decisions. In our age of technology, public information is readily available. Accessing information through public sources, however conscientiously, offers no special advantage in strategy or decision-making.

Information gained from private sources, via a network, is a different story. If you have access to unreported trends in your industry, the release date of emerging technologies, or knowledge about a company's hiring or promotion strategy, you can use that information to competitive advantage. Obviously, the more diverse your network, the more of this private information is available to you. You want to be connected to people of high integrity who have access to private information. The varying priorities and views you encounter in these relationships may sometimes make you uncomfortable, but you need some level of discomfort to grow and succeed, especially at higher levels of leadership.

2.   ACCESS TO DIVERSE SKILL SETS

Uzzi and Dunlap explain,

> Linus Pauling, one of only two people to win a Nobel
> Prize in two different areas, and considered one of the
> towering geniuses of the twentieth century, attributed
> his creative success not to his immense brainpower or
> luck, but to his diverse contacts: "The best way to have a
> good idea is have lots of ideas." While expertise has be-
> come more specialized during the past 15 years, organi-
> zational, product, and marketing issues have become
> more interdisciplinary, which means that individual suc-
> cess is tied to the ability to transcend natural skill limita-
> tions through others. Highly diverse network ties, there-
> fore, can help you develop more complete, creative, and
> unbiased views of issues. And when you trade infor-
> mation or skills with people whose experiences differ
> from your own, you provide one another with unique,
> exceptionally valuable resources.

3.   POWER

As organizations have become flatter over recent years, power
has become less about position and more about access to information. Again, think about what those who are positioned as
links among diverse networks have to offer. Others seek out
these individuals and want them on their teams and projects.
Information brokers link specialists who can work together to
solve problems, adapt to change, synthesize differing points of
view, and create value for customers.

Brian Uzzi and collaborators Yang Yang and Nitesh
Chawla wondered if the advantages of diverse networks might
be even more important for women than men. To find out, they
conducted a study to determine what types of networks helped

new female and male MBA graduates obtain executive leadership positions. In an article titled, "Research: Men and Women Need Different Kinds of Networks to Succeed," Uzzi reported:

> We found that men benefit not so much from size of network but from being *central* in the MBA student network—or connected to multiple "hubs," or people who have a lot of contacts across different groups of students.
>
> Women benefited in terms of post-MBA job placement from being central in the network too; but to achieve the executive positions with the higher levels of authority and pay they *also* had to have an inner circle of close female contacts, despite having similar qualifications to men, including education and work experience.

Regardless of gender, being central (a key link between networks) provides access to information about the job market, including who is hiring, what salaries those companies offer, opportunities for promotion, and how to best attract recruiters' attention.

While this information is largely public, a central position gives a candidate timely access to this information, which is widely scattered among students. But women also need private information to overcome the cultural and political hurdles they uniquely face when seeking executive leadership positions.

The research showed that women need an inner circle of close female contacts with whom they regularly connect. These contacts provide private information about an organization's receptivity and practices toward women leaders. This information can be critical in developing successful strategies for applying, interviewing, and negotiating for executive positions. Successful men have inner circles in their networks too, but the gender composition of those inner circles was not connected to job placement.

The statistics are compelling, pointing us once again to the importance of strategically developing and leveraging relationships:

> Women who were in the top quartile of centrality [in the MBA student network] and had a female–dominated inner circle of 1-3 women landed leadership positions that were 2.5 times higher in authority and pay than those of their female peers lacking this combination. In contrast, women who had networks that most resembled those of successful men (i.e., centrality but no female inner circle) were placed into leadership positions that were among the lowest in authority and pay.

> Women's success also depended on a certain kind of inner circle. The best inner circles for women were those in which the women were closely connected to each other but had minimal contacts in common. For example, if Jane is a second-year MBA student whose inner circle includes classmates Mary, Cindy and Reshma, but these three women each have networks with few overlapping contacts, then Jane will benefit not only from her three inner-circle-mates but also their non-overlapping contacts.

*****

If you are a woman who aspires to a leadership position, the life examples, perspectives, and research findings in this chapter deserve your attention. Making the move to higher levels of the organization, especially the move from individual contributor to leader, is a unique and stretching experience, even when the move matches your most-wanted career goal.

Purchasing WUI from Jean Otte was certainly a stretching experience for me. Jean sold the business to me and Nina Dougar, our CFO, with me as the majority owner. I had worked with Nina for many years under Jean's leadership. Now I needed to develop a different relationship with Nina as business partner—as well as with Jean as our founder.

Jean moved to an advisory role on our board, but she didn't automatically know how to step back and let me take the lead. By her own account, Jean didn't know how to be in a meeting "without sucking the air out of the room." I struggled to demonstrate my profound respect for Jean, who had been my mentor and an important role model for years, and my need to claim my own space. Frankly, to do my best as the organization's president and CEO, I needed Jean to get out of the way.

When Jean and I were in meetings together, she often tried to insert herself, and she seemed not to realize she was hampering my effectiveness. My initial reaction was to feel hurt or angry. After all, Jean had chosen to sell the business and make this transition.

While Jean was an incredible visionary and leader, I knew it was time for the organization to change. If Jean held sway, the organization would stay where it was instead of moving forward as it should as a result of new leadership.

As you can imagine, this situation caused short-term stress. It might have turned into a terrible experience for Jean, me, and WUI. But the open, direct, and authentic relationship that Jean and I had developed was the key to resolving the problem.

Over my years of working with Jean, I had welcomed her to challenge my thinking because it helped me make better informed decisions. I'm not saying it was always easy to be challenged, but I valued the openness we shared and the insights and perspectives that were unique to Jean. While we were similar in many ways, we would sometimes see situations from very different perspectives. Given that we were both strong in our beliefs, we had robust debates. We had developed a relationship that allowed us to have these heated discussions in such a way that helped us learn what the best outcome should be. Because of this, I was able to speak to Jean about what I was noticing and feeling, and we were able to hash out our relationship and roles in a productive way.

The reconfiguring of roles was not the only stretching dimension in this transition for me. Jean's experience as an executive was a critical component to her success in launching WUI. I did not have commensurate executive experience. Newly at the helm of WUI, I felt it was important for me to have the appropriate credentials to lead the organization.

As I considered our partners and the types of challenges and questions they had, I saw a need to gain greater evidence around WUI's learning models. We needed to ground our approach in cutting-edge research. Our programs had been designed and developed with input from our team and with partner feedback. Now, as we were looking forward, I wanted to make certain I was getting outside perspective, both via research and best practices from leading companies.

As you know, I decided to enroll in a program at the University of Pennsylvania. As the program participants were learning/business leaders from global organizations, this was opportunity to get an outside perspective into the work we were doing. Nina, Jean, and I made a plan for me to participate in the three-year program, which was comprised of weeklong classes in Philadelphia, coursework, and research. To be certain that the business needs of WUI continued to be met, I asked Jean to take on certain projects that allowed me to attend class without worry. With Nina and Jean's support, I was able to balance the needs of the business and the program.

I chose to do my research on the role of relationships for mid-career women. My knowledge base, relationships, and credibility in the eyes of our partners all increased dramatically as a result of my participation in the program at Penn. As I approach high-level decisions or ambiguous situations, I have a global network from which to gain insights and diverse perspectives. I also have early access to changing trends in the corporate and learning landscapes. All these things make me a better president and CEO.

Like other male and female leaders, I've changed my vantage point, responsibilities, and the way I show up as I've grown in my executive career. And like other male and female leaders, I've found it possible to maintain my authenticity along the way. I've flexed my style, not myself, while striving to be the most effective leader I can be. You can do the same.

CHAPTER 9

GIVING FEEDBACK
WITH GRACE AND CARE

We humans do not do well when someone whose inten-
tions are unclear tells us where we stand, how good we
"really" are, and what we must do to fix ourselves. We
excel only when people who know us and care about us
tell us what they experience and what they feel, and in
particular, when they see something within us that really
works.

— Marcus Buckingham and Ashley Goodall

Shifting to a leadership position requires you to mentor others, help them take calculated risks, give performance
feedback, and sponsor them for job changes that provide learning and growth experiences. In short, your role involves creating capacity in others to perform and grow into larger roles.
This aspect of your job begins with your earliest leadership
jobs and becomes more and more important as you go higher in
the organization.

This shift from doing the work to fostering growth in others can be as uncomfortable as it is necessary. It requires letting
go and letting others forge a path to accomplish tasks you'd

like to control. It requires honesty and difficult conversations when you might prefer to hide in your office.

So why mentor others? First, it is your job. Organizations can't grow unless their people expand their capacities. Second, becoming intentional about developing people is the ethical thing to do.

When asked why he invests in giving feedback to others, especially in the tricky environment between genders today, Jack Yurish says,

> I take the attitude that giving feedback is more honest and loving than withholding it. When you see someone who is doing something that's going to be injurious to their career, or even if they're dressing in a way that is not going to help them get on the promotability list, is it honest to avoid telling them because you don't want to upset them or get a negative response from them? Or is it more honest and loving to share feedback in a way that is helpful, allowing them the opportunity to see it as helpful to their career and act upon it?

Yurish does have an important clarification about the appropriate perspective from which to provide feedback: the foundation of any feedback must be the other person's career goals and aspirations. Yurish says,

> I always start with what the person wants to achieve in life as a career and as a person. One of the mistakes men often make is that they make assumptions. In working with women (or anyone, for that matter), if you really want to try to be helpful, you have to 1) understand who they are and what their aspirations are. If they have a particular aspiration for a particular job or function or whatever, you have to understand that clearly so that

you can 2) guide them in that direction with the right kind of information and resources.

When a person sees that specific input is going to be helpful to his or her goals, that person is more inclined to listen to the input and act upon it.

As leaders, we need to take time to reflect and make sure we come from such a place of service—and with a good dose of humility.

To illustrate, let's revisit Annie McKee's story. As accomplished as she is today, you know that McKee's professional journey did not begin on an auspicious note. With two young children and a husband who wasn't able to partner with her to provide for their family, McKee first scraped together a living, including cleaning, cooking, and ironing for a woman named Mary Burton. Having become an accountant in the 1960s, Burton was ahead of her time as a professional woman. Her example taught McKee lessons that endure to this day.

Burton managed to give feedback in a way that supported McKee and made her believe in herself, even at an extremely vulnerable point in her life. McKee says,

> Here I was, first young with no kids, and then young with kids, and poor. We were so poor that Mary bought us a Christmas tree one year because we could not afford one.
>
> Mary would gently remind me that I was smart and confident and able to do more than I was doing—while valuing what I did. I've been in jobs where people say, "Hey, you're really smart, you should be doing more than this." They said this while demeaning what I was doing—and that did not make me feel good or receptive. Mary did it differently. She never sat me down and said, "You should go to college and you should do this, and you should do

that." She instilled me with hope and a belief in myself and a belief in women as I watched her.

Years later, McKee made it through college with the help of other women who banded together as peer mentors under the guidance of a nun, Sister Anna. Then divorced with three small children, McKee believed she needed even more education to be able to support her family.

As McKee was beginning graduate school, Richard Boyatzis was just starting a professorship. McKee, who had been resisting the business world up until that point, felt sure she didn't have much in common with Boyatzis. She would never have picked him for a mentor; in fact, she decided it was best to stay clear of this particular professor. Here's how McKee tells the story:

> Well, guess what? Richard approached me as one human approaches another human. He was my professor while I sat in his classes, but the respect that he gave me for who I was, was absolutely genuine and real. It just felt so supportive. It was clear he wanted to mentor me; I knew that. By this time, I kind of knew it was because I was smart and hardworking, and all those good things. His stance, his being, was similar in many ways to Mary's and to Anna's, even though he was completely, radically different than either one of those people. I felt I could be mentored by Richard, I could be taught by Richard, and I wouldn't be losing my soul.

Now an accomplished and respected woman in a senior role, McKee is in the position of mentoring others. She hasn't forgotten the lessons she learned on the receiving end. She says,

People that I mentor may look up to me or think that what I've done is great. It's when we're able to let go of all that, on both sides, that we reach each other. And that's when movement happens. When we connect with human contact between one person and another in the most basic sense, movement happens.

It has always been important for me not to be seen as the trappings of my life, whether it was poverty, studenthood, or as a female in a man's world, as is the case so often in my field.

When I'm in a relationship with somebody, whether I'm learning from them or they're learning from me, the absence of projections is important. As an example, I'm thinking of a woman from Syria who got out of the country just as the war started. She ended up trapped in Saudi Arabia for four or five years before she finally got to the United States. It is tempting to see this person as a Muslim woman who was essentially imprisoned by her husband.

It is tempting to just see her as the trappings of her life, because they are so present, as I'm sure my poverty and my tired, single mom presence was so present and large. But that gets in the way. And it gets in the way of really understanding each other's experience and understanding the dignity of that human being who is sitting with you. We have to guard against that.

Even when we approach our job as mentors and sources of feedback with the best of motives and a healthy dose of humility, those on the receiving end don't necessarily know this. Many people have legitimate reasons to be guarded about trusting others.

So, for Tony Hunter and other experienced mentors, building trust is first on the agenda in establishing a new developmental relationship, particularly a cross-gender one. Hunter says he puts in a lot of up-front work by telling stories, letting mentees know they are in a safe harbor with him, and encouraging them to talk with other folks he has mentored. I love how Hunter expresses some of his rationale for this:

> I know I won't bat a thousand in how I convey my ideas, how direct I am, and whether I express empathy or not. I prepare when I'm getting ready for a mentoring session, especially with a female, but I'm not always going to be perfect. I think of the old Steven Covey advice: "Make deposits in the relationship bank so that when you make a withdrawal, you don't get your account closed."

> I call out specific things in an early session. For example, I let a person I'm mentoring know she can come to my office and vent. If that's what she wants to do, I'll listen and allow a place for her to vent. When you build trust, people can vent and not feel like they're being judged. They feel better and can get a better perspective.

> Then the other thing I say is, "I promise you that whatever we talk about I will keep between us, and I will always ask your permission. If I can help you in a situation, I will always ask you before I do anything on your behalf.

Who wouldn't find this kind of open and honest relationship extremely helpful? It allows for conversations in which a less senior person can bounce ideas and potential directions off a more senior person without feeling judged or one-down. In such situations, the best mentoring may come in the form of good questions and long pauses. It may also come in statements like "I wonder if you've considered this perspective . . ."

It may come in a suggestion to have conversations with a few other seasoned individuals—followed by an introduction to those individuals. In many cases, a person doesn't need advice as much as a variety of points of view. And sometimes that person needs encouragement to sleep on the matter for a few days.

ADVICE ON GIVING FEEDBACK
IN CROSS-GENDER RELATIONSHIPS

Because Tony Hunter has been mentoring and sponsoring women in WUI for nearly 20 years, it seemed fitting that I bring up with him the delicate issue of male/female mentoring relationships in today's tricky cultural environment.

From Hunter's perspective, we don't need to have long discussions about appropriate behavior. He said, "Men need to behave properly, and they know what that means."

When it comes to mentoring relationships with women, Hunter recommends a man examine his intentions. The sole purpose of such a relationship *must* be the woman's well-being, professional growth, and success. If any other intention exists, the man should not enter the relationship.

It's important that men understand, appreciate, and honor the delicate balance of *influencing* versus *leveraging power* in their interactions with female colleagues. Executives and leaders already have position power within their organization. With the added power that comes with being looked up to as a mentor, the delicate balance can quickly get skewed. Protégés put their mentors on a pedestal, and once again, it's critical that all mentors

keep the best interests of their protégés at the forefront. It is especially important for men to understand that every word and action sends a message about the relationship.

> The lines denoting the difference between a healthy profes-
> sional relationship and a personal one need to be kept clean
> and clear.
>
> Even in mixed-gender relationships of high integrity, both
> parties need to exercise an abundance of caution to ensure
> the optics don't suggest anything beyond a business rela-
> tionship. The optics matter, and they have power to hurt
> reputations. Savvy executives and professionals pay atten-
> tion to them.

In an article called "The Feedback Fallacy," Marcus Buckingham and Ashley Goodall warn against trends that suggest managers need to give feedback constantly, directly, and critically.
As we've seen earlier, critical feedback triggers a biological
threat response, which causes our brains to focus on surviving,
not learning. The authors say:

> Feedback is telling people what we think about their per-
> formance and how they should do it better—whether
> they're giving an effective presentation, leading a team,
> or creating a strategy. On that, the research is clear: Tell-
> ing people what we think of their performance doesn't
> help them thrive and excel, and telling people how we
> think they should improve actually *hinders* learning.

So, what *fosters* learning and growth? For starters, Buckingham and Goodall want us to make sure our underlying
mindset and approach is aligned with current research. We
need to do the following:

1. UNDERSTAND THAT WE ARE FALLIBLE
   AND LACKING IN OBJECTIVITY

When it comes to rating abstract qualities like business acu-
men, strategic thinking, and political savvy, we can't be relia-

ble. Our evaluations, in fact, typically say more about us than they do about the person on the receiving end of the rating. The authors say, "The only realm in which humans are an unimpeachable source of truth is that of their own feelings and experiences." All we can do is share our own feelings, experiences, and reactions—and those are valuable pieces of information in and of themselves.

2. FOCUS ON REINFORCING STRENGTHS AND SUCCESSES, RATHER THAN POINTING OUT WEAKNESSES AND FAILURES

Human beings learn best in areas where their brains are already the strongest, where they already have the most neurons and synaptic connections. We don't learn by starting from scratch; we learn by making connections with what is already there. Giving attention to someone's strengths acts as a catalyst for learning while focusing on a person's shortcomings impairs it. Effective feedback helps a person better understand his or her strengths and perhaps learn a subtle nuance to make good performance even better.

3. ACCEPT THAT EXCELLENCE IS ALMOST IMPOSSIBLE TO DEFINE

Excellent performance, while always the goal, is anything but clear cut. This is because excellence, by nature, is idiosyncratic and individualized. We can't dictate how excellence needs to look in someone else's performance, because excellence is, in Buckingham's and Goodall's words, "a natural, fluid, and intelligent expression of our best extremes. It can be cultivated, but it's unforced."

Of course, this book contains accounts of people learning from feedback that wasn't presented optimally, at least when measured against Buckingham and Goodall's recommendations. When I was in my first job and Don told me that every manager in the factory thought he could do my job, Don was not making an effort to reinforce one of my strengths, yet that feedback was profoundly helpful to me.

Susan Sobbott appreciates certain times when leaders were direct with her, even pointing out a mistake. For example, the woman who was running the small business division of American Express when Sobbott first arrived there gave some advice. One day, Sobbott walked into a meeting a minute or two late and sat on the outskirts of the room. During the meeting, the leader said, "Come sit at the table." Afterward, she gave Sobbott a lecture on how wrong it was to sit on the outskirts of the room. After all, if Susan wanted to have a voice, she needed to be at the table. She needed to claim her position.

And when Courtney Collins received harsh and abrupt feedback from an executive, she courageously worked to face and process the criticism. If we want to grow, we can't count on others to know how to communicate well.

When it's our turn to offer feedback, however, we would do well to heed the research and adopt best practices. Here are some suggestions from Buckingham and Goodall:

LOOK FOR OUTCOMES

Think of excellence as an outcome and look for it. For example, "Take note of when a prospect leans into a sales pitch or a project runs smoothly. Then turn to the team member who created the outcome and say, 'That. Yes, that!'" This interrupts the flow and causes the person to see an approach, behavior, or execution that demonstrated excellence. It's in context, immediate, and specific.

REPLAY YOUR INSTINCTIVE REACTIONS

Give feedback by describing your own experience in witnessing excellence. Describe what you saw and what you felt. This is both authentic and believable. Try a phrase like, "This is how that came across for me," or "This is what that made me think," or "Did you see what you did there?" As your honest reactions, such phrases, along with the details you share, are powerful. They are feedback, not judgments.

PERFORM A HIGHEST PRIORITY INTERRUPT

A friend of mine told me about a story her 5-year-old told her in the early days of kindergarten. The child explained that the class had been returning to the room after lunch. She said, "Matthew sat in my chair, and I said, 'It's okay, Matthew, you can sit in my chair."

The teacher interrupted the class to say in an excited voice, "Children, something wonderful just happened!" And the teacher explained to everyone how the child had shown kindness when the other child mistakenly took her chair. The teacher praised a child doing something right, both reinforcing it and using it as a positive example for the whole class.

Buckingham and Goodall point out that we have a natural instinct to use an interrupt strategy when things are going wrong. When there is a problem, especially involving a customer, it can be appropriate to stop, give feedback, and get the person involved to fix it. But be aware, the authors caution, that taking this action is only remediating; it will not cause the person to learn or get closer to excellence. On the other hand, catching someone doing something that really works (saying "Yes. Do more of that!") and stopping to dissect it will cause the person to learn:

> Her understanding of what excellence looks and feels like within her will become more vivid, her brain will become more receptive to new information and will make connections to other inputs found in other regions of her brain, and she will learn and grow and get better.

Interrupting for an opportunity like this is not only a positive step, the authors tell us it should be your highest priority interrupt.

EXPLORE THE PRESENT, PAST, AND FUTURE

Buckingham and Goodall outline a simple process for responding to a request for feedback on performance or what that person needs to do to get promoted.

In approaching you, this person is seeking to solve a problem or meet a goal in the present, so start in the present—but not with sage advice. Instead, begin by asking the person to tell you three things that are working for him right now. Getting the person to think about what's working, even if it is unrelated to the issue at hand, affects his or her brain chemistry in positive ways, opening the brain to new ways of thinking or acting.

Next, turn the person's attention to the past, because it's likely that he or she has encountered a similar issue before. Ask, "When you had a problem like this in the past, what did you do that worked?"

Finally, turn the person's attention to the future. Ask the person to tell you what he or she already knows must be done. You might share a few of your own experiences, but don't let your thinking get in the way. Assume the person already knows the solution. Your job is to simply help this person discover it.

Ask questions that lead to specific answers and action. For example, "What are a couple of actions you could take right now?"

*****

When a senior leader gives feedback that leads to better performance surrounding business outcomes, it is a gift to the receiver, no matter the gender. Research indicates, however, that men are more likely to get this type of feedback than women.

This may be particularly true in formal feedback sessions, in which male managers are uncomfortable pointing out challenges or developmental opportunities to women for fear of a negative or emotional reaction. In such situations, male managers are required to have the conversation, but they may deal with their discomfort by being vague.

In a *Harvard Business Review* article titled, "Research: Vague Feedback is Holding Women Back," Shelley Correll and Caroline Simard describe a study they conducted on a sample of performance evaluations across three high-tech companies and a professional services firm. They found that women consistently received less feedback tied to business outcomes than their male counterparts did.

> The vague feedback lets women know they are generally doing a good job, but it does not identify which specific actions are valued or the positive impact of their accomplishments. We also learned that vague feedback is correlated with lower performance review ratings for women—but not for men. In other words, vague feedback can specifically hold *women* back.

Correll and Simard's research suggests these trends may stem from unconscious bias. Because stereotypes emphasize women's caregiving abilities, reviewers are likely to attribute women's accomplishments to teamwork rather than leadership. They are less likely to acknowledge a woman's technical expertise and/or her contributions to the bottom line.

What's more, the developmental feedback women do receive tends to be overly focused on communication style—and negatively focused at that. For example, in a study of 200 performance reviews, Correll and Simard found that 76% of the women's reviews contained references to being "too aggressive." This same reference was contained in only 24% of the men's reviews.

Meanwhile, men received insightful and specific feedback about their technical skills and how to excel in areas deemed important by the company scorekeepers. Here is an example from one of the performance appraisals: "You need to deepen your domain knowledge in XYZ space. Once you have that understanding, you will be able to contribute to the design decisions that impact the customer."

To grow their careers, women need mentors to let them know where they excel, where they need to build skills and which technical projects they should pursue. It's a leader's job to provide this information. Nobody, of course, is suggesting this is easy. It is, as Jack Yurish would say, the moral thing to do.

Correll and Simard say,

> Necessary critical feedback can be difficult for a manager to offer anybody, but . . . it can be especially uncomfortable when it is given across a dimension of difference, such as gender, race, or age. When giving feedback to women, male managers may be especially worried about how the feedback will be received. This "protective hesitation"— the failure to give feedback due to worry that the recipient might be upset—is a critical barrier in having conversations necessary to advance women's careers.

They suggest the following five steps to level the playing field when providing performance reviews. These steps make sense for all developmental conversations, regardless of gender.

1. Before beginning evaluations, outline the specific criteria you will use to evaluate individuals. Identify the specific behaviors or results that demonstrate mastery—and use the same criteria for all employees at the same level.

2. Plan to discuss three specific business outcomes with each employee.

3. Tie feedback, whether positive or developmental, to business goals and outcomes. Be specific about behavior and outcomes.

4. When evaluating people in similar roles, give equal weight to technical accomplishments and capability. Provide the same level of detail for all.

5. Write reviews of similar lengths for all employees. This will help to provide a similar level of detail for all.

As leaders who are responsible to give feedback via formal reviews, it's good to remember that unconscious bias can taint our reviews. I appreciate the steps Correll and Simard outline, helping us to reduce bias as we approach those who work directly for us. As we approach others, it's important to remember that feedback has the power to wound as well as to foster growth. I'm especially grateful for the perspectives of Annie McKee and Jack Yurish. As long as we approach others with respect for their dignity, appreciation of their accomplishments, and in the context of helping them achieve their own goals, feedback is one of the greatest gifts we have to give.

CHAPTER 10

RELATIONSHIPS MATTER: WHERE DO YOU GO FROM HERE?

The best way to build a relationship is to give, rather than receive. Most importantly, make sure you're giving support to people who are asking for help. But also help people who are not asking but whom you think could benefit from you. Have those foundations in place so when the time comes that you need help, the relationships will be there. If that time never comes, you've made an investment in humanity and friendship.

— Susan Sobbott

As you know, when Jean Otte decided to launch WOMEN Unlimited, Inc., she reached out to her network and shared her vision. Without anything other than the conversations, she started the first program. When Jean later talked about this initial period in the business, she shared her vision to create a program that helped women become leaders.

The powerful part of Jean's story is *how* she did it. Jean had created a strong professional network. She reached out to individuals she knew and met with them. She also asked these individuals who else she should be speaking with. In other words, she leveraged her network to the max! Jean was un-afraid to ask for help, and she actively sought out people she felt could be helpful. Yes, Jean had an engaging personality and she was also very appreciative.

Jean also engaged those who were the initial sponsors to get feedback on their experience. Imagine creating something unique—at the time WUI launched, there was no similar offer-ing—and the feeling you might have as you asked your first customers for feedback.

Of course, Jean was thrilled to hear people share the as-pects of our work they found valuable. Others might not have probed past the compliments, but Jean did. She asked very spe-cific questions to find out what was not working or could be done better.

Jean was a role model for not taking critical feedback per-sonally. I was with her on occasions when folks gave her feed-back that evoked a reaction in me, only to see Jean ask more questions, seemingly unfazed.

One day, I asked Jean how she managed to stay so calm in such discussions. Jean shared that she knew if she reacted, she would not get the insight that was so important to grow her business.

Years later, when I bought the business from Jean, I decided to hire a consultant to conduct a market analysis. (I had noticed some resistance in the marketplace and wanted to know the cause.) Jean was with me in the meeting to discuss the findings.

The man who conducted the research was hesitant to get started. Jean and I grew concerned about what we were about to hear. We started asking, "Do the companies you spoke with not value what WUI does? Is there an issue with how we have designed our programs?" No, it wasn't either of these things.

Jean and I, frustrated and eager to understand, finally blurted out, "If the companies are saying they want what we are offering, rip the Band-Aid off and just tell us what's wrong!"

In the end, the analysis pointed to some things we needed to do to refresh our image—all good insights. We then had a great conversation about whether the man would have presented differently if he were speaking to two men.

These stories of Jean and the ways in which I learned from her over the years remind me of the profile of a strong leader that has emerged from my research, experience, and interviews. I shared this profile with you in Chapter 1. It seems right that we revisit it as we come to the end of this book. In many ways, we've come full circle.

1. VALUE RELATIONSHIPS

The fundamental attribute in the profile of a successful leader is *an appreciation that no one succeeds alone.* Successful leaders don't expect themselves to know everything, especially in today's complex and ever-changing environment. They see no shame in asking questions, asking for help, or requesting support. Those who know they cannot succeed on their own value relationships and the exchange of ideas, support, and resources. In short, they know that relationships matter, and invest in mutually supportive relationships as a matter of course.

2. INTENTIONALITY

Successful individuals are aware that they alone are responsible for their own careers. Rather than wait around for someone to notice and promote them, these individuals are *intentional* about where they want to go and the strategies needed to get there. They figure out where they can best contribute to an industry or organization and chart a path to get there. When appropriate, they take calculated risks to move themselves forward along their chosen path.

3.   CURIOSITY

While all the attributes in the profile are important, my favorite is *curiosity*. Perhaps this is because my earliest role model for curiosity was my mother. Jean, of course, was another tremendous role model for this trait. She constantly wanted to know what others thought. She developed a high level of skill at asking questions and seeking out information. As you've seen, Jean was fearless in soliciting feedback from our corporate partners—she knew neither she nor the business could perform at its best without it.

In a *Harvard Business Review* blog post, Tomas Chamorro-Premuzic claims that curiosity is as important as intelligence—and that we should be measuring potential leader's CQ (curiosity quotient) as well as their IQ (intellectual quotient) and EQ (emotional quotient). According to Chamorro-Premuzic, CQ is the ultimate tool to produce simple solutions for complex problems.

4.   SELF-AWARENESS

Strong leaders are curious about many things, including how others see them. They seek to identify gaps between how others perceive them and how they want to be seen. They put effort into growing their *self-awareness* and devoting time to mindfulness. This, as we've seen, results in a willingness to receive feedback, even when that feedback is difficult to hear. In order to grow in self-awareness, an individual must make a commitment to put aside defensiveness and evaluate feedback as objectively as possible.

5. PURPOSE AND PASSION

Jean Otte, like many powerful leaders, inspired others by her *purpose and passion to contribute.* Jean was all about helping women succeed—in a time when there were far fewer women in leadership positions than there are today. Strong leaders invest time and thought into discovering their talents and figuring out what career and position is right for them in terms of making the biggest possible contribution.

Jean's passion ignited mine as well as that of many others. Within the context of Jean's passion for helping women succeed, each team member at WUI pursues her unique role and passion. I see mine as helping others find true joy in their careers.

6. REALISM

Leaders who succeed are *realistic about organizational dynamics.* They learn that understanding and working with the rules of the game need not sully them. These leaders identify the scorekeepers in their organizations, and they work to influence those leaders. They uncover the formal and informal rules of their organizations, and they work within them in intentional ways, maintaining their integrity and authenticity even as they adjust the way they show up to match their positions.

Taken as a whole, this list of attributes may seem like a lot to process—like an impossible model against which to measure yourself. If so, I encourage you to take heart and simply begin by taking a single step forward. For me, accepting rather than rejecting a single piece of feedback from an honest colleague was enough to raise my awareness of how I needed to move forward.

I wonder what single step is right for you. It depends a great deal on who you are and where you are in your career journey. Perhaps your step is to begin asking questions that will build awareness about your performance and expanding your relationships. I'm not suggesting a big, audacious question such as, "Will you be my sponsor?" but a simple one such as, "I am experiencing this challenge. I'm thinking of handling it this way. Are you willing to tell me your thoughts?" Maybe the question you need to ask is even less risky, such as, "Can you tell me one way I could improve my next customer presentation?"

On the other hand, maybe your one step forward is to assess your readiness to create a developmental network for yourself—or to adjust your network now that your career has advanced. If so, review Chapter 3 to remind yourself of the steps that Kathy Kram recommends: 1) get to know yourself first; 2) know your career context; 3) enlist potential developers; and 4) regularly reassess and adjust. Remember, too, that all leaders need three types of networks: operational, personal, and strategic. Don't shortchange yourself by failing to build all three types.

Maybe your next right step is to take action to expand or diversify your network. If so, Chapter 4 is full of success stories and strategies. As I heard people's stories, I was often amazed at how many strategies to building a network are manageable and natural. There's no need to feel one-down as you reach out to others.

Perhaps it's time to face your hesitation, fear, or defensiveness in asking for or receiving feedback that might hurt. While feedback is a gift, it doesn't always feel that way. This is because negative feedback, even if well-intentioned, can literally trigger our biological fight-or-flight response. Managing this challenge begins with adopting a mindset that feedback is simply data you get to evaluate. It may or may not be valid.

Next, you need to manage your reactions. The stories in Chapter 5 will give you strategies to help you do that.

I hope I've convinced you that in order to own your career and achieve your goals, others need to see your contribution to the business. Maybe it's time for you to champion your own value. You might consider raising your hand for a visible cross-department project or make a lateral move so that you can become known more widely. A review of Chapter 6 will refresh your memory of what research has to say about why women stay out of the spotlight—and what you might do to move into it.

It might be time for you to take a big step—a strategic risk—to own your own career. What is one step you can take to strategically build your core skills, expand your responsibilities, or expand your network inside or outside your organization? I love the conversation between Jack Yurish and Jean Otte, recorded in Chapter 7. Yurish says,

> As we were discussing the concepts of WUI over many nights, Jean would repeatedly say, "Well, but I couldn't do that."
>
> I would say, "Why not?"
>
> Then, as we talked further, she would say, "Oh, I don't think that's possible."
>
> I would say, "Why not?"
>
> The question for me was always, "Why not?" For every objection Jean had, I would say, "Let's talk about it. Why not?"
>
> We kept chipping away at the objections. At one point, Jean said, "I'm never going back to New York."

Of course, New York is exactly where Jean went to start the program.

I'm so glad that Jean's objections didn't hold her back from realizing her dream. If fear of taking a risk is threatening to hold you back, revisit stories like this one in Chapter 7. They are stories of very human people who managed to find the courage to take the risk they needed to move forward.

Perhaps for you, like many women, the idea of navigating organizational politics makes you uncomfortable. You have a lifelong commitment to authenticity and have always avoided playing the game. If so, your next step is to summon your courage and figure out how to be strategic and authentic at the same time. You may have to change the way you show up, but you never have to compromise yourself or change who you are. If you fail to make the adjustment, you'll fail to give the best you have to offer as a leader.

Wherever you happen to be in your career journey, it's an appropriate time to give feedback and support to others. As you learn from those more senior to you, be supporting your peers and helping those who follow. The stories and advice in Chapter 9 will help you fill this role effectively and with grace.

That brings us to this final chapter. The stories and best practices I've been privileged to tell in these pages leave me profoundly confident that women leaders have the capacity to make wonderfully positive contributions to our organizations and our world. Yes, I know that women face real barriers in advancing in today's complex environment. There are layers upon layers to the problem, and we can become easily discouraged. I am not, however, discouraged. Women have the power to set high-level career goals and build the relationships as well as skills and experiences needed to get them there. Never forget that relationships matter, and that you control the size and composition of your own network. If you are ready to take control of your own career and contribute in big ways, reach out, ask a question, have a conversation, lend a perspective, lend a hand. It's time for action.

NOTES

CHAPTER 2

Ibarra, Herminia. "How Women Can Build Their Professional Networks." *Wall Street Journal*, May 20, 2018. https://www.wsj.com/articles/how-women-can-build-their-professional-networks-1526868480.

Mayo, Margarita. "The Gender Gap in Feedback and Self-Perception." *Harvard Business Review*, August 31, 2016. https://hbr.org/2016/08/the-gender-gap-in-feedback-and-self-perception.

CHAPTER 3

Levinson, Daniel J. *Seasons of a Man's Life.* New York: Ballantine Books, 1978.

Parker, Polly, Douglas T. Hall, and Kathy Kram. *Peer Coaching at Work: Principles and Practices.* California: Stanford Business Books, 2018.

Ibarra, Herminia, and Mark Lee Hunter. "How Leaders Create and Use Networks." *Harvard Business Review,* January 2007. https://hbr.org/2007/01/how-leaders-create-and-use-networks.

Kram, Kathy, and Monica C. Higgins. "A New Mindset on Mentoring: Creating Developmental Networks at Work." *MIT Sloan Management Review*, April 15, 2009.

https://www.bumc.bu.edu/facdev-medicine/files/2009/12/Kram-Higgins_A-New-Mindset-on-Mentoring.pdf.

Jordan, Sheila. *You Aren't Ruining Your Kids: A Positive Perspective on the Working Mom.* United States: Pittsburgh, Pennsylvania: inCredible Messages, 2018.

CHAPTER 4

Obama, Michelle. "Remarks by the First Lady at the National Mentoring Summit." Speech, Washington, DC, January 25, 2011. Obama White House Archives. https://obamawhitehouse.archives.gov/the-press-office/2011/01/25/remarks-first-lady-national-mentoring-summit.

Heen, Sheila, and Douglas Stone. *Thanks for the Feedback: The Science and Art of Receiving Feedback Well.* New York: Viking Press, 2014.

Heen, Sheila, Douglas Stone, and Brue Patton. *Difficult Conversations: How to Discuss What Matters Most.* 2nd ed. New York: Penguin Books, 2010.

Casciaro, Tiziana, Francesca Gino, and Maryam Kouchaki. "Learn to Love Networking." *Harvard Business Review*, May 2016. https://hbr.org/2016/05/learn-to-love-networking.

Nauiokas, Amy. "How to Diversify Your Professional Network." *Harvard Business Review*, August 29, 2018. https://hbr.org/2018/08/how-to-diversify-your-professional-network.

Johansson, Francis. *The Medici Effect: Breakthrough Insights at the Intersection of Ideas, Concepts, and Cultures.* Boston, Massachusetts: Harvard Business School Press, 2004.

CHAPTER 5

Bregman, Peter. "How to Ask for Feedback That Will Actually Help You." *Harvard Business Review,* December 5, 2014. https://hbr.org/2014/12/how-to-ask-for-feedback-that-will-actually-help-you.

Heen, Sheila, and Douglas Stone. *Thanks for the Feedback.*

Brown, Brené. *The Gifts of Imperfection: Let Go of Who You Think You're Supposed to Be and Embrace Who You Are.* Center City, Minnesota: Hazelden Publishing, 2010.

CHAPTER 6

Seddeek, Ash, and Leslie A. Rubin. *Meaning: How Leaders Create Meaning and Clarity During Times* of Crisis and Opportunity. United States: Pittsburgh, Pennsylvania: inCredible Messages Press, 2018.

Feder, Robert. "Former Tribune Publisher Tony Hunter Exits tronc." Robertfeder.com, December 8, 2016. https://www.robertfeder.com/2016/12/08/former-tribune-publisher-tony-hunter-exits-tronc/.

Fielding-Singh, Priya, Devon Magliozzi, and Swethaa Ballakrishnen. "Why Women Stay Out of the Spotlight at Work*."* *Harvard Business Review*, August 28, 2018. https://hbr.org/2018/08/why-women-stay-out-of-the-spotlight-at-work.

Ely, Robin, Pamela Stone, and Colleen Ammerman. "Rethink What You 'Know' about High-Achieving Women." *Harvard Business Review*, December 6, 2014. https://hbr.org/2014/12/rethink-what-you-know-about-high-achieving-women.

Chapter 7

Ettus, Samantha. "Inspiring Quotes From 100 Extraordinary Women." *Huff Post,* January 23, 2015, Updated Dec 6, 2017. https://www.huffpost.com/entry/100-quotes-from-100-extraordinary-women_b_6483622.

Parsons, Nancy. *Fresh Insights to End the Glass Ceiling.* United States: Leader Voice Publishers, August 2017.

Babcock, Linda, Maria Recalde, and Lise Vesterlund. "Why Women Volunteer for Tasks that Don't Lead to Promotions." *Harvard Business Review,* July 16, 2018. https://hbr.org/2018/07/why-women-volunteer-for-tasks-that-dont-lead-to-promotions.

Sandberg, Sheryl. *Lean In: Women, Work, and the Will to Lead.* New York: Alfred A. Knopf, 2013.

Chapter 8

Herminia Ibarra. "Why Strategic Networking Is Harder for Women." *Forbes,* April 8, 2016. https://www.forbes.com/sites/worldeconomicforum/2016/04/08/why-strategic-networking-is-harder-for-women/#3f0f93776c01.

McGreary, Johanna. "Blunt but Flexible." *Time International (South Pacific Edition),* February 17, 1997. Ebscohost. https://www.cnn.com/ALLPOLITICS/1997/02/10/time/albright/mcgeary.html.

Uzzi, Brian, and Shannon Dunlap. "How to Build Your Network." *Harvard Business Review*, December 2005. https://hbr.org/2005/12/how-to-build-your-network.

Uzzi, Brian. "Research: Men and Women Need Different Kinds of Networks to Succeed." *Harvard Business Review,*

February 25, 2019. https://hbr.org/2019/02/research-men-and-women-need-different-kinds-of-networks-to-succeed.

CHAPTER 9

Buckingham, Marcus, and Ashley Goodall. "The Feedback Fallacy." *Harvard Business Review*, March-April 2019. https://hbr.org/2019/03/the-feedback-fallacy.

Correll, Shelley, and Caroline Simard. "Research: Vague Feedback is Holding Women Back." *Harvard Business Review*, April 29, 2016. https://hbr.org/2016/04/research-vague-feedback-is-holding-women-back.

CHAPTER 10

Chamorro-Premuzic, Tomas. "Curiosity Is as Important as Intelligence." *Harvard Business Review*. August 27, 2014. https://hbr.org/2014/08/curiosity-is-as-important-as-intelligence.

ABOUT THE AUTHOR

As President and Chief Executive Officer of WOMEN Unlimited, Inc. (WUI), Dr. Rosina Racioppi spearheads her organization's initiatives to help Fortune 1000 companies cultivate the talent they need for ongoing growth and profitability. Under her leadership, WUI successfully partners with organizations across a wide range of industries to develop their high-potential women and build a pipeline of diverse and talented leaders.

By overseeing the management of programs and services nationwide, Dr. Racioppi is actively involved in helping organizations meet the challenges of a continually changing global economy. Additionally, she analyzes and develops new business opportunities, works with current Fortune 1000 partners to assess and update offerings to their high-potential women, and ensures that WUI is in sync with the needs of its present and potential partners.

Having worked with and then taken over the reins of WUI from its founder and chief mentor, Jean Otte, Dr. Racioppi has firsthand knowledge of the power of relationships to build careers and organizations in amazing ways. Dr. Racioppi's own career journey is peppered with incidents in which developmental relationships and thoughtful feedback played significant roles.

Dr. Racioppi earned her doctorate in education from the University of Pennsylvania. Her dissertation, "Women's Mentoring Wisdom," focuses on how women use and fail to use mentoring at the all-important mid-career level. She earned a Master of Science in education from the University of Pennsylvania, and a Bachelor of Science in Criminal Justice from Michigan State University. She is certified in the Hay Job Evaluation Process and the Crosby Total Management System.

Prior to joining WUI, Dr. Racioppi held executive management positions in human resources at Degussa Corporation, Nextran (a division of Baxter Corporation), and Beechwood Data Systems. She has over 25 years' experience in Organization Planning and Development, Compensation and Benefits, Training and Development, Safety, Quality Management, Staffing, and Employee Relations.

Dr. Racioppi is an active member of the Society of Human Resources Managers, The American Society of Training and Development, and The New Jersey Human Resources Planning Group. She served on the Advisory Council for the University of Pennsylvania CLO Alumni Network. She is a featured columnist for *Chief Learning Officer* magazine and a sought-after expert for many media sources, including *CEOworld Magazine, Fast Company, Forbes, TLNT, Thrive Global*, and business.com.